This Here Flesh

This Here Flesh

Spirituality, Liberation, and the Stories That Make Us

Cole Arthur Riley

CONVERGENT
NEW YORK

This is a work of nonfiction. Some names and identifying details have been changed.

Published in the United States by Convergent Books, an imprint of Random House, a division of Penguin Random House LLC, New York.

CONVERGENT BOOKS is a registered trademark and its C colophon is a trademark of Penguin Random House LLC.

Permissions credits are located on page 205.

LIBRARY OF CONGRESS CATALOGING-IN-PUBLICATION DATA
Names: Arthur Riley, Cole, author.
Title: This here flesh / Cole Arthur Riley.
Description: New York: Convergent, [2022] |
Includes bibliographical references. |
Identifiers: LCCN 2021044732 (print) | LCCN 2021044733 (ebook) |
ISBN 9780593239773 (hardcover) | ISBN 9780593239780 (ebook)
Subjects: LCSH: African Americans—Religion. | Spirituality—Christianity. |
Spiritual life—Christianity. | Storytelling—Religious aspects—Christianity.
Classification: LCC BR563.B53 A78 2022 (print) | LCC BR563.B53 (ebook) |
DDC 200.89/96073—dc23
LC record available at https://lccn.loc.gov/2021044732
LC ebook record available at https://lccn.loc.gov/2021044733

Printed in the United States of America on acid-free paper

crownpublishing.com

2 4 6 8 9 7 5 3

First Edition

Book design by Jo Anne Metsch

TO THE HOUSE ON CEMETERY LANE.

We're not afraid of you.

PREFACE

On Storied Contemplation

I have a favorite sound.

To be precise, it's not a singular sound but a multitude.

Have you ever stood in the presence of a tree and listened to the wind pass through its leaves? The roots and body stand defiant and unmoved. But listen. The branches stretch out their tongues and whisper *shhhhh*.

Trees make symphonies without their trunks ever moving, almost as if the stillness of their centers amplifies their sound. The tree may appear still, but if you look closer, you'll see that each leaf flails with breath. The tree may seem alone, but plow deep and you'll unearth its secret gnarled roots—the grotesque and the beautiful—creeping in the soil, reaching toward the ancestors.

Thomas Merton said, "No writing on the solitary, meditative dimensions of life can say anything that has not already been said better by the wind in the pine trees." I hold this close.

My spirituality has always been given to contemplation, even before anyone articulated for me exactly what "the contemplative" was. I was not raised in an overtly religious home; my spiritual formation now comes to me in memories—not creeds or doctrine, but the air we breathed, stories, myth, and a kind of attentiveness. From a young age, my siblings and I were allowed to travel deep into our interior worlds to become aware of ourselves, our loves, our beliefs. And still, my father demanded an unflinching awareness of our exterior worlds. *Where is home from here? What was the waitress's name? Where do we look when we're walking?* If a single phrase could be considered the mantra of our family, it would be *Pay attention.*

Later, in the arms of white intellectuals, much of what I absorbed of the contemplative life rested on demands of knowledge, silence, and solitude. I learned to read the words of dead men, and go on silent retreats, and "listen" alone in my room, all in hopes of hearing something true of God. These are practices that I'm not quick to sneer at, as they have often been co-opted from the wisdom of Eastern spiritualities and diluted. Still, I do not believe they alone tell the story of the contemplative life.

I wrote this book during the fall and winter of 2020, during the coronavirus pandemic. When I am finished, I will be in my fifteenth month of isolation, as I am one of the many immunocompromised who cannot test my fate with this virus. Apart from my husband, my days are spent in solitude, in a kind of silence and stillness. It has reminded me what an empty spiritual life will manifest from these virtues alone. I cannot sustain belief on my own. And I'm learning sometimes the most sacred thing to do is shout.

I used to think that Christian contemplation was reserved for white men who leave copies of C. S. Lewis's letters strewn about and know a great deal about coffee and beard oils. If this is you, there is room for you here. But I am interested in reclaiming a contemplation that is not exclusive to whiteness, intellectualism, ableism, or mere hobby. And as a Black woman, I am disinterested in any call to spirituality that divorces my mind from my body, voice, or people. To suggest a form of faith that tells me to sit down alone and be quiet? It does not rest easy on the bones. It is a shadow of true contemplative life, and it would do violence to my Black-woman soul.

In Toni Morrison's novel *Beloved,* Baby Suggs, the matriarch, gathers all of her people in the Clearing. Everyone is standing on the edges, waiting in the trees for her to begin to preach. And she says, "Let the children come," and they all scurry to the center, and she tells them, "Let your mothers hear you laugh," and they laugh. And she calls the men to come down and says, "Let your wives and children see you dance." And they do. And finally, she calls the women to the center and says, "'Cry . . . For the living and the dead. Just cry.' And without covering their eyes the women let loose." And they all get tangled up in each other, and the men are crying, and the women are dancing, and the children are laughing, until eventually, they all collapse in the grass together to hear Baby Suggs give a sermon. "In this here place, we flesh; flesh that weeps, laughs; flesh that dances on bare feet in grass," it starts. Morrison writes, "She did not tell them . . . to go and sin no more."

She calls them to awaken to their stories. And then she leads them in this sacred cry of the body.

More on this to come. But this literary moment of intergenerational, dignity-affirming, embodied liberation is my model for spirituality to date.

When I think of my ancestors who lived in chains, I often wonder what sacred defiance lived in their minds while their bodies were being dominated by another. For the field and plow and whip can certainly affect the mind, but they cannot possess it. What hidden things of old crouched in the corners of my great-great-great-great-grandmother's consciousness as she stood in the cotton fields? What stories, dreams, and beliefs about God hugged the crevices of her brain? The oppressor has no power in those deep and secret places. Much of Black spirituality while enslaved had to live and breathe in these crevices, every vale holy ground. A faith that depended on the interior life.

In this way, contemplative spirituality is in Black blood. But it is not a spirituality of disembodied, solitary intellectual musing. It is a way of being together in "the Clearing" with God. And we get there by descending into the stories that reside in our bodies. For me, most simply, contemplative spirituality is a fidelity to beholding the divine in all things. In the field, on the walk home, sitting under the oak tree that hugs my house. A sacred attention.

And as we pay attention, we make a home out of paradox, not just in what we believe but also in the very act of living itself. Stillness that we would move. Silence that we would speak. I believe this to be a spirituality our world—overtaken with dislocation, noise, and unrest—so desperately needs.

So I write these pages in solitude but tethered to those to whom I belong and who in some manner belong to me. I sit in silence but attuned to the whispers of my ancestors and all who have formed me. And I *inhale-exhale* in stillness, liberated from the frenzied bondage of this world and protecting the breath of my body.

It is here I will admit I was wary of beginning with the image of the tree. I agonized over it as I drank my evening tea and while I was supposed to be paying attention in meetings. Would I really use a tree—this image that has been used so often, used to the point of death—to begin this book?

Until it occurred to me that it was very fitting. This is not a book of new things or ideas; my thoughts have been thought before. It is more remembrance than revelation, more maybes than certainty. And there is sparse novelty. Much of what you'll find here is old and even, I hope, familiar. But I mean to go deep into the old, that it might find some manner of resurrection by virtue of coming from my own blood and bone. Not *What is the tree?* but *What is the tree to me? When did I first touch its bark, and how does it move me? What would I call that shade of green? What do I hear when I listen?*

This is a book of contemplative storytelling. The pages you hold are where the stories that have formed me across generations meet our common practice of beholding the divine. *Feel now,* they are wet with tears. *Look* how they glisten like my skin in sun, and they bear the grooves of many scars. As you cradle these pages, it is my sincere hope that they might serve as conduits for mystery, liberation, and the very face of God.

CONTENTS

This Here Flesh

ONE

Dignity

A baby bursts out of a great Black womb saying, *It is what it is what it is* and he is my father.

My gramma used to say, *Oh, chile, when your daddy came outta me, he tried to take his whole house with him*. He cleaved to her insides like he knew what was his to have.

My father was born smooth. He glides and sways when he walks, cuts his hands through the air in meaningful arcs when he talks, like he's in a ballet. I've never seen the top of his head because I've never seen him look down. He told me from a very young age, *Keep your head up, relax those shoulders, look at that skin shine*. He told me that Black was beautiful. It seemed to me that he was a man who would never think to apologize for his existence. Some people are born knowing their worth.

I was an anxious and insecure child. I'd tiptoe around with my shoulders cupping my ears like a perpetual flinch. I believe my father saw this in me and did what he could to drown out whatever primordial voice had told me to fold up my personhood into something small and negligible.

Every morning, he'd squeeze my sister and me in between his legs as he methodically parted our hair and laid grease on our scalps. He'd spend what felt like hours propped up in his chair, leaving us with braids stretching in all directions, barrettes and ballies gripping the thick black curls. When he finished, he would lick both thumbs and press them against our shaggy eyebrows and say, *You look good, honey. Do you feel good?* This was our ritual. And in time, it formed us.

Toni Morrison's novel *Beloved* has become a sacred text to me. It tells the story of a family, once enslaved, now making their way in freedom as they dwell with the ghost-force that haunts their home. When Morrison takes us back to the Clearing, the family's matriarch, Baby Suggs, preaches a message to all the women and the men and the little children who lie in the grass after dancing, laughing and crying together. After leading them in a practice of liberation with their bodies, Baby Suggs says this:

> In this here place, we flesh; flesh that weeps, laughs; flesh that dances on bare feet in grass. Love it. Love it hard. Yonder they do not love your flesh. They despise it. They don't love your eyes; they'd just as soon pick em out. No more do they love the skin on your back. Yonder they flay it. And O my people they do not love your hands. Those they only use, tie, bind, chop off and leave empty. Love your hands! Love them. Raise them up and kiss them. Touch others with them, pat them together, stroke them on your face 'cause they don't love that either.

This is necessary ritual. From the womb, we must repeat with regularity that to love ourselves is to survive. I believe that is what my father wanted for me and knew I would so desperately need: a tool for survival, the truth of my dignity named like a mercy new each morning.

I cannot say with precision when I came to believe him—or if I ever truly have—but the knowledge began with my father and Toni Morrison and stretches back into God. The origin story of the world and the dark and stars that hold it is one of dignity. The divine is in us.

When I first heard that all humans were created in the image of God, I pictured God with a million eyes and a million noses and a million mouths. It was horrifying. What did this mean, all humans? If God walked in the garden of Eden, whose two legs did he walk with? Did they look like mine, with knees black and ashy?

It is not wholly unusual for individuals or cultures to imagine God as being like them in some way. Perhaps this is because we lack an imagination for a being who loves us and doesn't resemble us. Things that are unlike us strike us as unsafe. When I encounter the unfamiliar—a new food, a stranger on the train—I may be intrigued, but I am nearly always cautious. I've no frame of reference for how it might hurt me, what compels it to violence or tenderness. If God is like me, then perhaps she becomes more predictable. Safer. But when we force our picture of God on another, or when God is presented as singular, we tend to colonize the image of God in others.

As a default, I imagine God as a white man. Even now that I know the tragedy and the lie in the image, it seems to be branded on my soul. I used to feel guilty because of this, but what else should be expected of me with all the stained glass and oil paintings? Does the church truly believe that God might look as much like me—gapped teeth and skin like glistening leather—as a white male? It has damaged many to think that the holiest being that ever was looks precisely like the man who kept our ancestors in bondage.

It takes time to undo the whiteness of God. When I speak of whiteness, I am referring not to the mere existence of a person in a particular body; I am referring to the historic, systemic, and sociological patterns that have oppressed, killed, abducted, abused, and discredited those who do not exist in a particular body. Whiteness is a force. It moves in religion in the same manner it moves in any sphere of life. In art, it might look like the glory of the American Western film and the lie of white bravado. In global development, the lie of the white savior. These are spiritual afflictions in and of themselves, but in religious communities, when whiteness becomes inseparable from the character of God, you'll find customs such as evangelism equated with conquering, but admissible under the guise of "love." You'll find guilt-driven spirituality, which is obsessed with alleviating guilt and becoming "clean"—for whiteness always carries the memory of what it has done to those in bodies of color, and guilt is its primary tormentor. The irony, of course, is that this guilt cannot be relieved save by a rending of whiteness from the image of God (which the force of whiteness will never do).

In order to rend whiteness from the face of God, we must do more than make new images. We have to persist in observing and naming all the ways this force has obscured the face and character of God. The God I've known does not dominate; he kneels and washes his enemies' feet. God does not make himself hero; he heals and works miracles both publicly and privately.

We also have to expand our understanding of how other cultures and peoples contain the divine. Does God slap the tambourine like my auntie? Do they put butter and salt in their grits?

Some theologies say it is not an individual but a collective people who bear the image of God. I quite like this, because it means we need a diversity of people to reflect God more fully. Anything less and the image becomes pixelated and grainy, still beautiful but lacking clarity. If God really is three parts in one like they say, it means that God's wholeness is in a multitude.

I do not know if God meant to confer value on us by creating us in their own image, but they had to have known it would at least be one outcome. How can anyone who is made to bear likeness to the maker of the cosmos be anything less than glory? This is inherent dignity.

I do find it peculiar that humans have come to wield this over the rest of creation as though we are somehow superior. I don't believe this to be the case. Sometimes I wonder if we knelt down and put our ear to the ground, it would whisper up to us, *Yes, you were made in the image of God, but God made you of me.* We've grown numb to the idea that we ourselves are made of the dust, mysteriously connected to the goodness of the creation that surrounds us.

Perhaps the more superior we believe ourselves to be to creation, the less like God we become. But if we embrace *shalom*—the idea that everything is suspended in a delicate balance between the atoms that make me and the tree and the bird and the sky—if we embrace the beauty of all creation, we find our own beauty magnified. And what is shalom but dignity stretched out like a blanket over the cosmos?

. . .

You know when the rain is pounding against your house and you curl up to listen to it make music, and the wind is drumming against the windows and the only thing that seems to be keeping them from shattering or collapsing in on you is the walls that they are sandwiched in between? My gramma is the storm *and* the walls.

When God made her, he covered her in rich brown velvet—skin so soft you find yourself stroking it more for your comfort than for hers. And when she stretches those soft limbs over you, she splays herself open and lets it all fall on you like a weighted blanket. Hers is a heaviness that soothes.

And there is nothing like her voice. It doesn't come from her throat like the rest of ours. It comes from her eyes. The words creep up behind her retinas. Every syllable coils around her pupils, and it's only ever poetry.

I don't know if her father ever told her she was beautiful, but I know he did not tell her about the second family he had two floors up in the same apartment building in the Bronx. The deception broke her mother, and my gramma and her sister were sent to live with distant relatives on a farm in Pennsylvania.

The people on that farm knew nothing of her velvet. A woman and a man whose precise relation to her remains unknown to this day. The woman who was not my gramma's mother used to tell her that she saw the devil in her high forehead, that she could tell just by looking that he had left his mark on her. My gramma doesn't know what it is that made them hate her so immediately.

In the mornings, they would make her and her sister kneel on hardwood floors and recite the scriptures. And after whatever form their torture took in the evenings, the woman and man who were not their father and not their mother would grab their faces and make them say, *We love you, Mommy, we love you, Daddy,* in unison.

There will always be those who expend a great deal of effort trying to manipulate someone into believing there's something in their reflection that isn't truly there. These are dangerous and desperate souls. Yet for all their trying, dignity was not and is not something that can be taken. Glory can't be unborn.

The devil didn't make anyone, and I don't think he has the power to unmake anyone. Our walk to liberation requires us to parse truth from trick. And to ask ourselves, What does evil have to gain in tricking us into believing we are anything less than glorious?

I would venture to guess it swallows our belonging first; after all, a person does not wish to be seen if they believe they are ugly. We hide our faces and settle down in the treacherous place of *nowhere*. And then it colonizes our body, knowing we will flee from it out of deep shame and embarrassment. Self-hatred moves in. It makes a mockery of our limbs, twisting and contorting them for its own means. And last, I believe, it steals our love. For who can accept love that they do not believe exists for them? Those who believe love is a scarcity are less prone to give it away freely.

I don't have many certainties about God. I do have many hopes. Chief among them is that it's true what they say: that God is love, is made of love, and looks at the faces of you and me and my gramma and, without hesitation or demand, delights.

. . .

In my early twenties, when I lived in Pittsburgh, I would often eat with a group of people who lived under the ramp to Bigelow Boulevard. We'd go into this hot dog place on Forbes Avenue or eat on sidewalks with our bums perched on upside-down buckets. I'd steal glances at their shoes or their fingernails caked with dirt and feel sad, but the kind of sadness that doesn't require anything from you. And I'd ask them question after question like I was interviewing the most important soul in the world. Maybe I was without knowing it.

Mars, glassy eyed and sun scorched, would turn a suspicious look on me and ask why I wasn't eating with my friends, with people my own age. He was in his early fifties and had two daughters my age, whose names he would always beg me to guess. I never did. And I never honestly answered his question. I can say now that I liked eating with them in part because I was too afraid to talk with my peers in classes and hallways, and perhaps in part because I thought this ritual made me interesting and kind. But soon I began coming because of the stories they held. The things they knew, the way they spoke. How Mars licked his teeth to keep from showing them when he was busting a smile. How Case let her words fall from her mouth out of order and then reassembled them again on a second try. I fell in love with some, and I remained terrified of others. It was a complicated awakening.

I once heard the activist John Perkins say, "You don't give dignity, you affirm it." I wish somebody had told me that as I sat cross-legged under those bridges or on sidewalks with bucket lids digging into my behind. I wish somebody had told me that I wasn't restoring these people. I wasn't restoring anything, save maybe myself. Even after five years of soggy sandwiches and piles of french fries and laughter and loss, some part of me still believed that I was giving these men and women dignity, and for that I am ashamed.

Our societies and communities have a way of grinding up and serving out dignity in portions based on our own human ideals and idols. In the history of the white Western world, you can trace a perversion of dignity in the name of usefulness. You are no longer the image of God, you are currency.

We cannot help but entwine our concept of dignity with how much a person can do. The sick, the elderly, the disabled, the neurodivergent, my sweet cousin on the autism spectrum—we tend to assign a lesser social value to those whose "doing" cannot be enslaved into a given output. We should look to them as sacred guides out of the bondage of productivity. Instead, we withhold social status and capital, and we neglect to acknowledge that theirs is a liberation we can learn from.

I'm afraid to know what my lived experiences really tell of what I believe about dignity. I suspect one day we'll have to account for all those we and our systems push to the perimeters. Who would dare pluck a single hair from the face of God? We are the fools.

For this reason, I disagree with those who say we bear the image of God only, or even primarily, by living out our faith in our labor. The thought is reductive, and it evidences that we are content to exclude those who will never work, who may never speak, who no longer make or do. Their image-bearing is not dispensable; it is essential.

Our dignity may involve our doing, but it is foremost in our very being—our tears and emotions, our bodies lying in the grass, our scabs healing. I try to remember that Eve and Adam bore the image of God before they did anything at all. This is very mysterious to me, and it must be protected.

. . .

Because of what we've made of dignity, it can be difficult, if not impossible, to believe in it.

When I was eight years old, before I could make sense of why I fled the other children on the playground and lied about having friends, my hair began to turn gray. Coarse white strands shriveled up on the crown of my head without invitation, politely wrapping themselves around their black peers and strangling them in the night. It was an invasion. And the attention was agonizing. Every day I'd sit squirming and rocking in my desk, head bowed like a monk praying for my own invisibility. The gaze of Alex Demarco at my back. He'd only pointed out a hair once, but the moment stuck to me. I asked my teacher if I could switch to the empty desk in the back row, knowing there I could exhale. She said no.

By the time I turned eleven, I would spend ages in front of the mirror parting my hair just right so that as little white as possible was visible. One night, we were all going out and my family was waiting downstairs for me to finish parting. Eventually, my dad sent everyone to wait in the car and came to the bottom of the stairs and called for me.

When he asked how much longer I'd be, all of the shame that had crusted over my muscles from years of parting combusted. I threw a fit. I don't remember the details surrounding it, apart from a comb thrown against my brother's door. I mainly recall the episode by the memory of my father's face, which had a calm blankness that only made my own body, flailing and loud, more of a spectacle. When my crying softened, I finally said, feeling more embarrassed than before, *I can't do this anymore.* And then, with certainty, *I have to dye my hair.*

My father's response, his face, still lives in me. He calmly asked me to come down from the stairs, and the low sound waves from his voice slid under my feet and flew me from that top stair to where he stood. He tucked my head into his chest, sowed a kiss into my hair, and just said, *Okay, honey. We can dye your hair.* I was so addled that my tears dried up, and I didn't say another word. He summoned my hair into a bun, and we walked to the car together.

On the day the world began to die, God became a seamstress. This is the moment in the Bible that I wish we talked about more often. When Eve and Adam eat from the tree, and decay and despair begin to creep in, when they learn to hide from their own bodies, when they learn to hide from each other—no one ever told me the story of a God who kneels and makes clothes out of animal skin for them.

I remember many conversations about the doom and consequence imparted by God after humans ate from that tree. I learned of the curses, too, and could maybe even recite them. But no one ever told me of the tenderness of this moment. It makes me question the tone of everything that surrounds it.

In the garden, when shame had replaced Eve's and Adam's dignity, God became a seamstress. He took the skin off of his creation to make something that would allow humans to stand in the presence of their maker and one another again. Isn't it strange that God didn't just tell Adam and Eve to come out of hiding and stop being silly, because he's the one who made them and has seen every part of them? He doesn't say that in the story, or at least we do not know if he did. But we do know that God went to great lengths to help them stand unashamed.

Sometimes you can't talk someone into believing their dignity. You do what you can to make a person feel unashamed of themselves, and you hope in time they'll believe in their beauty all on their own.

That day on the stairs, my father could've very well tried to convince me that I was beautiful, begged me to believe that my gray hair was okay. But I think he knew that in order to stand in the presence of myself and others, he needed to allow for the unnecessary. The strange thing is, we never did buy the hair dye. In fact, I never asked about it again. By the time I was in high school, the white began to go away all on its own.

. . .

I used to want hair that slid straight down my spine like a golden cape. I used to want skin that burned red in the sun. But I've always loved the way my body moves when my hand is on a ballet barre. I love that my voice shakes easily and that I am skeptical to a fault. My father's pride sticks to my skin, and

I've absorbed it slowly like the cocoa butter he'd lather on us in the evenings before bed.

People say we are unworthy of salvation. I disagree. Perhaps we are very much worth saving. It seems to me that God is making miracles to free us from the shame that haunts us. Maybe the same hand that made garments for a trembling Adam and Eve is doing everything he can that we might come a little closer. I pray his stitches hold.

Our liberation begins with the irrevocable belief that we are worthy to be liberated, that we are worthy of a life that does not degrade us but honors our whole selves. When you believe in your dignity, or at least someone else does, it becomes more difficult to remain content with the bondage with which you have become so acquainted. You begin to wonder what you were meant for.

So bare your teeth as you smile, grease that scalp, relax those shoulders—hold your arms like their weight is in glory. You have been made.

TWO

Place

Long long ago, the birds you now see in the sky used to dwell in the bowels of the earth. Here, underneath us, they were scattered at birth and would spend their days squirming and scooting their way back to each other. Their wings, which they did not then know were wings, would flare out and press up against the walls of their tunnels, making it very difficult for them. Until one day, the sparrow and the swallow found each other. And I have to tell you, when their beaks cracked against each other just right, they heard a voice—from inside or outside, they could not tell—but it said to them then, *This is not the way*. And for reasons still unknown even to them, at that moment they looked in each other's beady little bird eyes and began to sing. Their song pierced the earth and everything began to crack right open. They scuttled their way up and up and up until the air caught their wings. And here is a secret: Did you know that birds do not land because they are tired? It is a remembrance. They know and have always known that their liberation depends on their ability to recall the ground.

. . .

When my father moved from New York City to Pittsburgh as a little boy, he says he got out of that old stick-shift Pinto, looked up, and couldn't stop staring. He just stood there squinting at all these cords and ropes hung from weathered tree trunks, wondering how Pittsburgh got all the green trees *and* these strange bare ones with rubber necklaces. *Power lines,* he said, describing it years later with a smirk that still contained some sadness. *In awe of power lines.*

Where he was from, these things were buried underground, and you might've never known they were there. They left Inwood just before Manhattan was suffocated by rosy cheeks and elegized in alabaster. They left when it still was breathing, but not enough to keep all four of them alive. For my gramma and the three tiny Black bodies she made, Pittsburgh was not the promised land but an exile.

Before this, my father had never really considered a world distinct from NYC. My gramma had explained they were moving, but he still imagined Pennsylvania with the subway and the Macy's Thanksgiving Day Parade and bagel shops on every corner. He had no imagination for elsewhere. A place where the pizza was shit. Where it was *yinz* and not *you guys*. When he saw those power lines for the first time, my father felt the vexation of something unraveling before him. To him, this was the first and ugly miracle of his displacement.

When I think of all that has formed me, I find myself drifting toward an articulation of people and circumstances. I'll tell you about what schools I attended and what parents raised me. But ask me to remember, and I'm on our old living room couch, smelling musty cigarettes and Murphy's Oil. I'm at the bakery on the Boulevard, pinching powdered pączkis. I'm sitting on a greasy kitchen counter with my stepmom staring down at me like I'm just getting free—the hot, salty crisp of latkes tingling with the cool sweetness of applesauce on my tongue.

It took time for me to accept that *where* we are has as much to do with our formation as *with whom* and *during what*. Place is the one thing that always is. We are always somewhere. I have been without people but never without place. Perhaps that is why it is so easy to become numb to it.

Isn't it something that in Genesis, God makes a home for things before God makes the thing? Not the fish first but the sea. Not the bird first but the sky. Not the human first but the garden. I like to think of God hunched over in the garden, fingernails hugging the brown soil, mighty hands cradling mud like it's the last flame in a windstorm. A God who says, *Not out of my own womb but out of this here dust will I make you*. Place has always been the thing that made us. We cannot escape being formed by it.

. . .

If you've suffered an anxiety attack, maybe you've encountered the grounding techniques of the five senses. *What's one thing you smell? Tell me two things you hear.* There is a mysterious entanglement between our welfare and our capacity to ground ourselves in a particular place. We are meant to be connected to our where, to the sensory experience of it. The simple beholding of place can slow your heart and steady your breath. It is quite the protective force.

I used to romanticize a nomadic existence. I used to think it was a requisite for "finding myself"—to travel around untethered until I stumbled upon a realness in me. It makes me wince to think that I thought I could learn myself by untethering. I'm very skeptical of this today.

For those of us whose sense of place speaks more of trauma than of belonging, it is understandable to think that the sole and sacred solution would be to belong nowhere at all. But this is alienation masquerading as freedom. It is a dangerous conflation. French philosopher and mystic Simone Weil said, "To be rooted is perhaps the most important and least recognized need of the human soul." Alienation and trauma of place are best met not with dislocation but with belonging, with a defiant rootedness, even if those roots stretch out to new and safer places.

My gramma says that in her twenties she was looking for peace and found it back in Harlem. As a child, her Manhattan-born soul had been exiled and transplanted to rural Pennsylvania before she knew where *where* was. *We were the Black family that lived down Cemetery Lane.* A place marred by death, surrounded by white people who were pleased with them in the way you can be pleased with your supper not being too spicy. *Negroes who knew their place.*

When she finally returned to the city, the ground shook beneath her for days, but her insides were still like pond water. She got off the A train and a man who looked like her was blowing a sax while his friend slapped a makeshift drum and sang out to her. It was a homecoming. And she leaned against the cold wall underground, letting the sound pulse around her. People moved past her like she was the wall, and maybe in ways she was, but not in the sad way—in the no-longer-a-spectacle way. She says New York City allowed her to get lost. *Listen, nobody knew if inside I was screaming or steady. I just was. I was a part of everything.* I suppose there is a safety in that. She was running from a man who had long mistaken obsession for love, and also from a sadness that stalked her when she was alone. I think she needed to get lost at first; I won't criticize her for that. Maybe getting lost let her be found on her terms. It offered a different kind of healing. A place to exhale.

To find a manner of anonymity, to experience that dreadful thing we call "blending in," can be a kind of haven. It is not to become untethered but to become a part of. To walk a street apprehending you are one small refrain in a holy cacophony, and as the place becomes more familiar, your own selfhood becomes more lucid.

There in the place of her origin, my gramma became new. Out of a graffiti-clad womb, singing songs in the subway. *Anytime I need to be born again,* she says, *I just go back to Harlem.*

. . .

I was sitting in McDonald's with my first Bible-study leader when I told her I didn't want Jesus in my heart. I was in my first year at the University of Pittsburgh and she, her last. She was gorgeous to me, even exposed to the fluorescent light rattling around us, but she spoke like the incarnation of a Hallmark card, which both aggravated and saddened me. I told her

I wanted God out there doing something, nodding to the street beyond the glass window. Why confined to a heart? She tried to defuse a look on her face by sipping on coffee that tasted like ash. I, embarrassed (whether on my behalf or hers, I did not know), began alternating peeling my bare legs off of the plastic booth to fill in the silence between us. Until finally she said, *That's where you're changed,* pointing to her heart not mine. And I didn't have the courage to say, *I like my heart just fine.* She motioned toward our fluorescent canopy and back to her chest. *For eternal life, God looks to the heart,* she said. And I couldn't tell her I had no desire to live forever.

As someone who is made of more doubt than faith, I find that Christians tend to want to talk to me about salvation. They seem quite concerned with the future of my faith, but they make the mistake of showing little interest in my present conditions. If asked to choose, I want a God who is someplace. Not just in "the heart," but God standing on Fifth and Lothrop—God beyond the glass. I don't just want to be rescued; I want to be taken someplace safe and good.

I think of Abraham's descendants leaving the promised land and being forced into bondage. God didn't raise up Moses just to free them from Pharaoh. They were liberated *to* somewhere. They left their chains and began making their way back home. What healing can manifest when place is restored, when those once dislocated from their home are delivered into it once again. It seems to me God's promise was always a place. A liberation born of location.

And such a freedom does not unfold in a vacuum but stretches out through those who have known a place before us.

This is what they don't tell you. You might think Abraham's promise from God begins with him, but before Abram, there lived a man named Terah. Terah took his family and set out toward Canaan, but for reasons unknown to us, he settled somewhere along the way and never saw the end of his journey. Yet, years later, his son Abram would, by the mouth of God, set out on a journey to a promised land, a land we now know as Canaan. Abram's promise did not occur in a vacuum. Whether he knew it or not, it remained connected to his father's journey. Our question is not only *What is this place to me?* but also *What has this place been to those before me and those who made me?*

I do not know from where my ancestors were abducted. I cannot tell you what the air smells like there. I don't know what sound the waves and soil speak. These things were stolen from me as they were from them. I think it is one of the deepest evils to become a thief of place, to make someone a stranger to their home, and then mark their relationship to the land by bondage instead of love. To steal place has less to do with power than with hatred. How much must one hate oneself and one's life and one's own land to run around chasing everyone else's? I used to think colonization was about ego, and maybe it is. But maybe it's not that the oppressors think they're worthy of more but that they believe their present self is, in fact, worthless. It's the work of people incapable of perceiving their dignity without attempting to diminish someone else's. It is no surprise to me then that these same powers, in the end, care so little for the land they are desperate to conquer. It was never about love or curiosity or care but a violent act of self-soothing.

I am mystified when I read stories of enslaved people who liberated themselves with the hope of owning and caring for their own land someday. Didn't they hate the cotton that pricked their bloodied fingers raw? Wouldn't they have cursed the sugarcane as they sliced through it again and again, feeling their lower backs gnarl? They gave their bodies for a place that didn't belong to them and to which they did not belong. I could understand if their bondage and demonic tethering to such land would drive them to a hatred of it. In mystery, it seems many found glimpses of freedom in it. Love, maybe. I am learning from this.

I hope God really is preparing a place for us. When God talks about getting her house ready, is she expecting us all at once? Does she have a gate, and if so, does she keep it open all through the night? Maybe there she will tell me the secrets of where I come from. She'll pull me into the kitchen just before grace and whisper all the secret things once stolen from me. All the places that I'm made of and don't yet know it. There I will learn the site of my soul. And we'll saunter back to the banquet fuller and more whole than I've known.

. . .

It was a red brick palace to me. It had two windows pushing out of the roof like eyes squinting in the dark. White vinyl casing framed the door in an arch. The doorbell actually worked, and the walkway was a million tiny stones. And it wasn't alone. Where I'm from, houses are close enough to each other that they touch in the wind. It was tight, like it would never be able to take a deep breath. But that didn't keep pride from swelling in my chest when my father knelt down and said, *It's home. It's ours.* As a little girl, I did not easily believe that something that felt so tall could belong to us.

As we got older, it slowly occurred to me that its spaciousness was more in comparison than in reality. There were seasons when we crammed eight people in that three-bedroom palace on Milan Avenue. We sat shoulder to shoulder, inhaling each other's exhales, pretending not to hear conversations we were never meant to hear. We crammed secrets in between each brick. Lean in and hear the laughter still stored safe. Ask the mortar what our wailing sounds like.

Then one day, from right there on the seam of the curb, I'm looking at four white pieces of paper clasping the front door. I'm twenty-one, and I see those papers, which I did not have the courage to read but which I knew spelled tragedy, and before I even knew I was moving, I turned and got back in the car. If my father ever did tell me we lost our house, if he ever explained the word *bankrupt,* I cannot remember the conversation now. It seemed that the knowledge of the loss punctured my subconscious in the night and slowly came awake until there were no questions left to ask. The papers did not surprise me, but they haunted me.

Eight years later, I came across a different house three hundred miles away from my genesis. Its limed red brick seemed ancient to me, ivy crawling up its spine. It was built in 1840 and never knew a gutter, so from the front you can see its brick belly swollen from time and rain. An oak tree and a maple tree frame its sides, towering higher than the house and reminding everyone who owns what. And behind it, just past the apple grove, sits a barn whose body looks pristine but whose floor is split open as though one day it arched its back and yawned so hard its diaphragm cracked right open. The house came with eight acres, which once were orchards.

And it called to me. I hope it's not too dramatic to say it seemed to call me by name.

We knew we could never afford it, but my husband and I would drive there after work in the evenings and hover just around the driveway, trying to steal peeks of it through the hedges. I saved a picture of that swollen brick belly and made it my phone background. We've since admitted it could have been a fiery pit inside and we still would've found a way to love it. And we watched for almost a year as, slowly, the asking price dwindled under the weight of rejection.

Even after we closed on it, it never felt as if it belonged to us. But my own sense of belonging became magnified. It was like something was restored in me. Its age began to settle on my skin as I thought of 1840 and what my ancestors would make of this brown-skinned girl descendant belonging to a place not out of bondage but out of love. To know that when I bend down in the reeds, pruning the path to the pond back to life, I do so of my own love and volition. To know that, at a time when the transatlantic abduction, enslavement, and purchase of Black bodies was occurring, God was preparing a place. A place for this little Black girl from Pittsburgh. Other days, I think of the white hands that laid and first owned these bricks and wonder what they would think of me. What they're whispering about us from the grave. I walk defiant through the halls and imagine them squirming. It's a kind of liberation, really.

Yes, it creaks at night, and the barn howls, but it is safe and it's a good place to grow things and be free. I am reconciled to the land by this place. And I have known no greater reconciliation to date.

We named the place Wisewood—in part because it had previously been named Marble Orchards, after Silas Marble, in 1820, and we didn't like the idea of adopting the name of a man who might've hated me or my Blackness or our love. Too timid to name it after ourselves, we chose a name that spoke to our aspiration: Wisewood. A place where we might be formed in wisdom and reconnect with the land. But we chose the name before we articulated the aspiration. I turn to my husband and say, *What will we call it?* And he says, much quicker than he says most things, *Wisewood.* These things are mysteries.

And we named it in part because it keeps us from getting too accustomed to saying *our house* or *our land.* We had learned from the native Onondaga tribe, who dwelled on the land long before Silas Marble was unjustly granted it for serving in the war, that believing yourself a possessor of the land is a damaging practice. I believe them. My ownership of the apple grove or barn or brick is an illusion that I chiefly entertain as a societal formality; or rather, my ownership does not mean what you think it means. The land I live on is not mine to have, but mine to nurture. I am responsible. A few months ago we bought a brush hog and began making paths in the reeds and charting out where we'll plant trees. We plant them knowing we may never see them grown enough to bear fruit. That we might be dead or elsewhere before we can sit under the shade of the pine by the pond. This is okay. I have known that my devotion to this place rests on my willingness to release any pretense that it belongs to me more than it is making me.

Ask me what I'm made of and I'll tell you to look down.

Me? I'm that Pittsburgh dirt. Knees black like the smoke

from the steel mills, which coated everybody's lungs without permission. Tears stank like the Monongahela River. I walked the Boulevard like I named it.

Now find me in the apple grove. Taste the tart of my flesh and wince. Climb through reeds with me till we meet the pond. Listen to the symphony of frogs croak out their weathered lullaby. I am still being made.

Do you know the promised land? Tasted the milk and honey on a sagging tongue?

I know a place.

THREE

Wonder

I have holes in my eyes. About a year ago, a doctor said it as plain as that. *You know about the holes?* I did not.

Apparently they are not uncommon, but I have enough of them that the doctors are all concerned. I am concerned. No one wants to think of decay in themselves.

There I lay—scratchy grass and soft earth wriggling around my little body as I looked up at the sky. Slow and chubby, there wasn't a game of tag I could keep up in. In the middle of the game, I would lurch over to the other side of the yard and collapse like a dead thing as the other kids ran around me, skipping over my motionless limbs. My eyelids would come awake slowly, finding the sky as I was resurrected. And I'd look up and just stare.

Then one day I learned to move my eyes in and out of focus. As I did so, it felt like I was witnessing a mask rip from the cosmos. In focus: clouds and blue, perfectly beautiful and ordinary. Out of focus: hundreds of minuscule clear floating bubbles suspended in the space between. I thought I was seeing air.

I wrestled my sister to the ground. *Look, there.* She squirmed and squinted. *Tell me you see the air.* She did not, which made me think I had special powers, and maybe I did. I try not to let the knowledge of my eye holes steal this magic now. For in actuality, I was simply seeing my own eye—floaters and shadows and flashes of light. It was still beauty to me. Now, a solemn magic. Some wonders have a way of holding us even in the deterioration of our present world. We must protect this.

Have you ever watched a three-year-old blow the wisps off a dandelion for the first time? Children are made of awe. We have much to learn from them, but we seldom aim to. When we encounter the freedom of a child, we can choose to participate in their liberation or we can grow to resent the freedom in them. The words *childish* and *juvenile* are made derogatory as we become overly concerned with the serious. It is a feigned superiority. The tragedy is that as we distance ourselves from the delight of our youth, we become increasingly prone to disillusionment. Wonder and beauty are not precise cures for disillusionment, but they certainly can stave off the despair of it. To reclaim the awe of our child-selves, to allow ourselves to be taken by the beauty of a thing, allows goodness to take up the space it's often denied in our interior worlds.

My first friend who was mine was a girl called Boo. "Mine" in that, before her, the only friends I had came to me by association with my sister, who was charming and popular enough to have friends left over to donate to me out of sympathy. This was enough for me then. Until the day Boo glided up to me at recess, pressed a spoon into my chest, and said, *Let's go to the fields.* And I went. Skipping so close behind her I had to dodge the plastic Kuhn's bag she had wrapped around her wrist. When we got to the middle of the deserted field, she lifted the bag and tore it open with her teeth. A jar of chocolate icing fell to the earth. I picked something crusty off the spoon and we ate. Legs crossed under us and knees touching, making shapes of the space between us. *This is our ceremony,* I said. *Yes, a ceremony,* Boo said, pinching the roots of her braids and whipping them over the icing in a circle.

It began like that. Knee to knee in an empty field, eating icing and clinking spoons. We began collecting seeds from helicopters fallen from trees. We'd grind them up and blow the dust into each other's hearts. Boo would cartwheel around me until the clouds whispered the secret of the day. *They say you are an angel.* And we laughed and bowed. *They say you'll be a dancer.* And we crossed our hearts. Our ceremonies ended with a whistle—fake, because neither of us could actually whistle. But to us it was real.

Until the day we had visitors. Three of them standing over us with their hips popped. They called us weird and "lame." They called us disgusting little babies. And the next day, Boo didn't bring a spoon for me. After that, I just sat by myself against the demountables, reading books and trying to forget being magic.

As we grow older, the "serious" becomes a simulacrum for wisdom and even honor. Impoverished by the honor withheld from us in childhood, we become very willing participants in a kind of spiritual maturation that honors the profound and grave, even at the expense of the simple and beautiful. In fact, the path to wonder is not sophistication or intellect or articulation; it is a clock wound backward. It is foolish, excessive. Two girls in a field flicking icing to the clouds. It's when you, as my family would say, *play too much*. The wonder I've known squeals in delight and trembles in terror. It waits for the clouds to whisper back.

. . .

People who truly know how to wonder don't expend a great deal of energy talking about it; they are off catching snowflakes on hot tongues. They're folding themselves in half to smell the sweet potatoes in the oven just one more time. I no longer try to convince someone of the delight of soup dumplings; I take them to Dim Sum Garden on Race Street in Philly and let them watch me slurp. I let the steaming miracle broth run down my face and lap it up in remembrance.

I think awe is an exercise, both a doing and a being. It is a spiritual muscle of our humanity that we can only keep from atrophying if we exercise it habitually. I sit in the clearing behind Wisewood listening to the song of the barn swallows mix with the sound of cars speeding by. I watch the milk current through my tea and the little leaves dance free from their pouch. I linger in the mirror and I don't look away. I trace the shadows hugging my lips and I don't look away. Awe is not a lens through which to see the world but our sole path to seeing. Any other lens is not a lens but a veil. And I've come to believe that our beholding—seeing the veils of this world peeled back again and again, if only for a moment—is no small form of salvation.

When I speak of wonder, I mean the practice of beholding the beautiful. Beholding the majestic—the snow-capped Himalayas, the sun setting on the sea—but also the perfectly mundane—that soap bubble reflecting your kitchen, the oxidized underbelly of that stainless steel pan. More than the grand beauties of our lives, wonder is about having the presence to pay attention to the commonplace. It could be said that to find beauty in the ordinary is a deeper exercise than climbing to the mountaintop.

When people or groups become too enamored with mountaintops, we should ask ourselves whether their euphoria comes from love or from the experience of supremacy. For example, whiteness, as a sociological force and practice, loves mountaintops. Being born of an appetite not for flourishing but for domination, it loves the ascent, the conquering. It will tell you about the view from there, but be assured that it is only its view of itself that rouses its spirit. It is about bravado and triumph.

There is nothing wrong with climbing the mountain, but bravado tends to drown out the sound of wonder. Perhaps you've known that person who devours beauty as if it belongs to them. It is a possessive wonder. It eats not to delight but to collect, trade, and boast. It consumes beauty to grow in ego, not in love. It climbs mountains to gain ownership, not to gain freedom.

I've climbed to 13,000 feet in the Himalayas, and when I think of it now, I very rarely find myself drawn back to the memory of a peak. I think of myself stopping somewhere along the way to watch a girl pick purple flowers sprung from snow. I'm listening to the Sherpa hum what sounds like Rihanna as he floats from rock to rock and I'm breathing hard as hell. I'm bowing. *Namaste*. I'm stealing glances at the tops of heads as I pass by the people in each village, and they bow too. *Namaste*.

To encounter the holy in the ordinary is to find God in the liminal—in spaces where we might subconsciously exclude it, including the sensory moments that are often illegibly spiritual.

When I was twenty-two, I boarded an unreasonably small plane to Nome, Alaska, and went to volunteer with the annual Iditarod Trail Sled Dog Race. The historic trail, much of which was once a trade route for Alaska Natives, was made famous after mushers with teams of sled dogs raced a serum to a remote village in the pits of a diphtheria outbreak. Now, each year, dozens of teams compete in a dogsled race to commemorate the journey from Anchorage to Nome.

I was working the lot overnight, scuttling around in the dark to keep my toes from turning to ice, when the winning musher and team of dogs came tearing through the finish line. I helped as the race vets examined the dogs. We walked them around as the doctors paid attention to how they moved. We slithered off their poop-caked dog booties. We helped bed them down, breaking apart straw bales and making nests in the snow. Sled dogs don't look like they do in the movies. They were small and wet and perfectly ordinary looking.

When I tell people I helped bed down the winning dogs of the 2014 Iditarod, their eyes get a particular shine to them. It reads like quite the grand adventure for a Black girl from Pittsburgh. And in its own way, it was. But this is the story from Nome that has settled into my skin: There I am, sitting on the porch of a rusting youth center with a friend and a local Inupiaq girl who can't have been older than twelve. We ignore the brown snow-slush coating the porch as we kick our legs over the side and brace our chins on the cold of the metal railing that wraps the perimeter of the porch. The girl is in the middle, holding her phone up like an offering, and our cheeks are all but touching as we lean into the screen and watch one video again and again—a parody of Psy's 2012 hit "Gangnam Style" that re-creates the entire song's music video using the game *Minecraft,* changing the iconic chorus to "Minecraft style."

To our right, the frozen expanse of the Bering Sea. Above us, powder leaks from the sky. And three very different humans squeal and pitch our voices two octaves too low as we sing out "Minecraft Style" like it's as important as "Ave Maria." This I will not forget. Lips cracking, bellies burning, snow sliding down my pants as I rocked back in laughter. It was one of those rare occasions that I knew was becoming a part of me as I lived it. The moment wasn't just happiness, though that was a quality of it. It was a kind of pleasure that made me feel a part of something—where beauty meets belonging.

When I talk about Alaska, no one really cares about this moment. It's simple and childish. To me, it was a miracle. The northern lights are one thing, but when I die, tell them that I went to Nome, Alaska, only to find God in a *Minecraft* parody.

This past winter, I made my husband lie in our backyard with me and look up. There was snow a few inches deep, and we were supposed to be covering up wood with the tarp to keep it dry. I was embarrassed to ask him. *Just for a second.* I wanted to see if he could see the air. He couldn't, but we lay there anyway, like forgotten rag dolls, and he let me tell him how the tiny clear things moved and popped around us. There are more of them now, but I don't let myself lie as long. A minute. And we went back to the wood and a conversation about the injustice of urban air quality. There was work to do.

If you want to know if you've forgotten how to marvel, try staring at something beautiful for five minutes and see where your mind goes.

. . .

"Taste and see that the LORD is good" (Psalm 34:8)—The Bible talks of knowing God as though it's closer to dinner and a movie than any three-point sermon.

What does it mean that our knowledge of the spiritual is deeply entwined with the sensory? That it is bodily? Double Dutch and the sound of braids and beads clacking together. The soft prickle of grass on bare feet. These are connections that require us to attune ourselves to our bodies.

When my father was in fifth grade, he signed up for a day program at school run by Alvin Ailey American Dance Theater. He was only trying to get out of class, but he ended up being asked to do one of their short residencies for kids in urban centers. *I can't tell you why I said yes. Boredom, maybe. I wasn't a dancer.*

But he's in class on the first day, and he gets brave, and all of a sudden, he hits a jeté like he's not ashamed of it, and the whole room stops as he levitates in the air. *Man, when I tell you I could fly back then . . .* He is suspended in the air like that for so long, his teachers have time to pay attention to every part of him. And as they're delighting and he's still flying, he has time to really take account of himself. His thin limbs stretching to the ends of the earth, his big globe eyes blinking back at him in the mirror like stars in a constellation. He says he felt the muscles around his knees become mighty. *I didn't know my body could do the things that it did.*

When he finally landed, it was the next day, and he was both terrified and proud. In awe of his body, he never saw it the same again. Years later, when he was in the army, doubled over on the twenty-mile march, fearing he couldn't take another step, he remembered this: the resilience, the strength, the beauty of his once-tiny body. And it's his own constellation that comes over to him and stands him upright again. He says, *It's not arrogant to wow yourself every once in a while. It's not arrogance, it's just paying attention.*

Wonder includes the capacity to be in awe of humanity, even your own. It allows us to jettison the dangerous belief that things worthy of wonder can only be located on nature hikes and scenic overlooks. This can distract us from the beauty flowing through us daily. For every second that our organs and bones sustain us is a miracle. When those bones heal, when our wounds scab over, this is our call to marvel at our bodies—their regeneration, their stability or frailty. This grows our sense of dignity. To be able to marvel at the face of our neighbor with the same awe we have for the mountaintop, the sunlight refracting—this manner of vision is what will keep us from destroying each other.

Our caution is to not become those who focus on beauty in order to dismiss tragedy or to disguise feelings of their own inadequacy. When we ourselves feel ugly and insignificant, or the pain of the world feels unbearable, it can be very comforting to talk of mountains and sunsets. We train our focus on beauty here or there—this poem, that architecture—because it is easier than bearing witness to our own story. We begin to gravitate not toward beauty but toward illusion. In this state, you are not approaching what you seek. You are running from your own face. But this is not the way of wonder. Wonder requires a person not to forget themselves but to feel themselves so acutely that their connectedness to every created thing comes into focus. In sacred awe, we are a part of the story.

For my father and his bony, levitating limbs, the wonder of his body pushed back the lie of a Black-boy monster. Practicing wonder is a powerful tool against despair. It works nearly the same muscles as hope, in that you find yourself believing in goodness and beauty even when the evidence gives you every reason to believe that goodness and beauty are void. This can feel like a risk to those of us who have had our dreams colonized, who have known the devastation of hope unfulfilled. I once heard the Japanese artist Makoto Fujimura say, "The most courageous thing we can do as a people is to behold." This gave me great empathy for those who have lost their wonder. For myself. We are not to blame for what the world has so relentlessly tried to crush in us, but we are endangered because of it.

Swiss theologian Hans Urs von Balthasar writes:

> Our situation today shows that beauty demands for itself at least as much courage and decision as do truth and goodness, and she will not allow herself to be separated and banned from her two sisters without taking them along with herself in an act of mysterious ven-

> geance. We can be sure that whoever sneers at her name as if she were the ornament of a bourgeois past—whether he admits it or not—can no longer pray and soon will no longer be able to love.

When we grow accustomed to neglecting beauty, we eventually become creatures of hatred. We lose our imagination—a virtue to which wonder is helplessly tied. Why care for barren land? Why advocate for justice in a system predicated on injustice? We become so accustomed to that bitter taste that we can taste nothing else. Slowly, even mirrors feel like an oppression. We become unable to conceive of anything worthwhile in our own image until we empty ourselves of all beauty and turn against our own bodies in disgust.

This is a path that ends in numbness. It is disillusionment with the chains of this world that leads us to become numb to them, accustomed to a life of burden as our appetite for liberation wanes.

When we wonder, we loosen the cords that restrain our love. And the people most in love with a thing are prone to become its fiercest protectors.

. . .

We have found ourselves too busy for beauty. We spin our bodies into chaos with the habits and expectations of the dominating culture, giving and doing and working. Do not blame yourself for that buzzing terror in the back of your mind; it was injected there at the site of our ancestors' enslavement. It takes work to undo that, especially when the oppressor still holds the whip today, ushering us into sixty-hour workweeks and minimum-wage jobs, dangling the hope of security in front of those of us who the system ensures will never have enough.

And once we name that we do not have enough, the system convinces us that it is our task to do more. We live depleted of that rest which is the only reliable gateway to wonder. We inhabit an economy of power that views wonder and awe as frivolities or naïveté, distractions on the path to liberation. Our remedy is precisely what our ailment derides. Wonder helps us get free.

I used to think our neglect of wonder was a function of being numb. It took longer for me to admit that this numbness was the result of trauma and disillusionment. When you become accustomed to pain, it is not unusual to, consciously or subconsciously, habitually weaken your capacity to experience pain. But as we become less perceptive of pain, we lose touch with other sensations as well—awe and delight included. As psychological wisdom explains, it is difficult to control the targets of our numbing.

With *The Color Purple,* Alice Walker taught me that wonder doesn't dismiss pain; it brings us out of numbness. Celie, a young girl who was told her whole life that she was ugly, learns about the godliness of beauty from Shug, her husband's mistress. Shug tells Celie, "I think it pisses God off if you walk by the color purple in a field somewhere and don't notice it." The story seemed to me more tragic than beautiful. But Walker knew Celie and Shug could not be reduced. Celie's life was more than a grotesque collection of traumas. She learned the language of wonder. And allowing for this awe in her did not diminish the pain of her story, it made her more human.

After my father tore her wide open, he lay on my gramma's heaving chest, still wearing her insides so you couldn't make out what was his flesh and what was hers. She says she looked down at him and was changed. *I was outside of myself,* she says. *I was a part of a miracle.* This was the moment she realized she was free to create beautiful things, and be beautiful herself.

She used to sing in church growing up, but when you're overworked and barely making it, it's hard to make time for loves. But when my father was born, she began singing again—not in church, but it was still a resurrection. Beauty has a way of multiplying itself. My gramma used to believe that her only role in this life would be devil. The woman and man who raised her convinced her she was born a bearer of the ugly, and that the beautiful things were despite her, never because of her. If she had never birthed a single child, I believe God would've still made a way for her to break free of this, but this is how it happened for her. A child whose beauty she couldn't easily deny.

To be a human who resembles the divine is to become responsible for the beautiful, for its observance, its protection, and its creation. It is a challenge to believe that this right is ours.

Wonder, then, is a force of liberation. It makes sense of what our souls inherently know we were meant for. Every mundane glimpse is salve on a wound, instructions for how to set the bone right again. If you really want to get free, find God on the subway. Find God in the soap bubble.

Me? I meet God in the taste of my gramma's chicken. I hear God in the raspy leather of Nina Simone's voice. I see the face of God in the bony teenager bagging my groceries. And why shouldn't I? My faith is held together by wonder—by every defiant commitment to presence and paying attention. I cannot tell you with precision what makes the sun set, but I can tell you how those colors, blurred together, calm my head and change my breath. I will die knowing I lived a faith that changed my breathing. A faith that made me believe I could see air.

FOUR

Calling

I always know when I'm dreaming. They're called lucid dreams, and I used to think it was the only way. It is a rare night when I—leaping from building to building, hiding from men in white masks, standing on the bridge as I watch the bolts shiver out one by one—do not eventually apprehend that I am asleep. Once I have, I can often make decisions and change the path of the dream altogether. When I leap, I choose if I land or plummet. When I am found, I can hide again and again until I find that precise corner that no man will ever look into. And when the bridge begins to sway, I decide if I wail in terror or sway along with it, humming with my hands in the air.

Apparently, the frequency of my lucid dreaming is rare. I used to believe it was a realness in me, that I knew without trying what was real and what was not. But what makes our dreams any less real? Somewhere within me, that bridge is falling.

When I told him about my dreaming, my brother sucked his teeth and said, *Man, you live and sleep in control. I want to know how to know.* What I didn't say then but felt with some degree of agony was that I wanted to know how to *not* know; how to feel like there is a calling from outside of you driving you toward that door and you walk through it like there is no other way. There is a certain comfort in a fate that is outside of yourself. Sometimes you just want to float and believe you are floating. Sometimes you want to believe the dream. I'm not one given to belief.

. . .

There's a story in the Bible of God calling Samuel so clearly he thinks it's the priest Eli calling out from bed. He hears a voice and goes to Eli three times before Eli finally tells him it's God doing the calling. When I first heard this, I thought how interesting it is that the question was not *What do I hear?* but *Who is calling?*

When I first began going to church, I couldn't believe how casually people spoke of hearing a calling from God. To them, it seemed as ordinary as having your mom on speed dial. A God who simply tells you to move abroad, or change jobs, or get married, or be single. I resented this for quite some time. That God would spend her time talking to people about which state to live in but would not rouse herself to tell me that she is real or that I am loved. It weighs on you as a kind of injustice that God would call some so distinctly and precisely and leave the rest of us to replay our own dreams five times a night just so we know which corner to hide in.

I'm not convinced I will ever hear from God in the way others have. My first instinct is to doubt the authenticity of their claims. I am patient with this instinct in me, but it becomes problematic when I begin silently mocking the "hearer" as if they are a menace merely for believing in something. It is too easy to erect these walls. *Did God really say . . . ?*

My first prayer was into a purple plastic toy megaphone. I even went into the closet to do it, in case God was shy like me. At the time, I received no perceptible reply. It has taken time for me to understand that what I am craving has perhaps been provided in other ways.

I've never heard God tell me to pick up a pen and write, but my father pressed my cheeks between his palms, pinching one of my poems in between his forefinger and a cigarillo, and whispered, *Don't forget this: You're going to write like you read*. And maybe it was God who knew that one night I would find that navy hardcover book with the silver foil lettering underneath our coffee table. And maybe he knew I would peel open its cover and find my gramma's words on the first page, one of her poems in an anthology. I held that book like it was a sacred text.

It did not feel like the world stopped spinning. I did not "hear" anything or feel like something was being communicated to me. But now when I retell that memory, I imagine something akin to the scene in *Harry Potter and the Sorcerer's Stone* when Harry chooses his wand, or rather, it chooses him. Some callings come to you only in memory. Some come only on the mouth of someone you trust. Some don't need to be heard in order to be lived. And not all calls come from outside of you.

. . .

Our questions of calling tend to be more aspirational than introspective. We spend a jarring amount of time asking young people what jobs they might have one day, compared to how often we ask them what is true of them right now. Both questions are worth asking, but I do wonder what I would've found true about myself earlier if someone had asked. The question of calling is not primarily a question of what we might become, but a question of what is already true—not least of which is what is true about the self.

Ask me what I want to be, but not before you ask me who I want to be. Ask me who I want to be, but not before you ask me the more searing question of who I am. Many of us will go to great lengths trying to answer this question without awareness of it. From horoscopes and the Enneagram to the social archetypes of the high school cafeteria, we are desperate for ways to make sense of who we are in relation to the world. It's troubling that the answer would not be immediately clear to us. But there are parts of us we've managed to hide even from ourselves.

Have you ever told a lie and then forgot it was a lie? When you tell a story for long enough, you begin to believe it. We adorn ourselves with any number of distractions from self. We embrace mirages in response to cues from the outside that we are not safe, loved, or welcomed. For example, if you have been hurting for long enough, you may find protection in the illusion of bravado or stoicism. Or if you have witnessed a person deemed undesirable for their neediness, you might learn to reject any part of yourself that stirs a memory of them. Haunted, you resolve that you will never be like them, and make vows against needs you do in fact have.

The sinister thing about the whole charade is that we seldom find true belonging in a masked or miraged state. Often, it's just the opposite. We don't forget the feeling of our own faces. Any love we receive while wearing the mask only affirms the belief that unmasked, we are indeed unlovable. Our shame is not resolved. It expands. Any affirmation we receive as mirages only keeps our true selves lurking in empty corridors, longing for touch. Illusions of self do not merely make for lonely souls; they make for hated ones.

For this reason, the process of knowing the self should be relentless. It will always be worth asking what is really true of us, for each day we live, we do so with deeper longings for acceptance, and the risk of alienation can cause us to dissociate from the truth of ourselves. Would you believe I have known seasons in which even the cadence of my voice has changed so that I might belong to a group of people whose stories and thoughts and ways were never anything like mine? But each year I know love and belonging—a love that doesn't require sacrifice at the altar of acceptance—I become more of who I already am. I am liberated into what Merton calls my "true self." I believe this is my deepest calling.

This doesn't mean I won't be called into new things or experience spiritual calls to change or grow. But even with the things I will become, I am called to them because on some deep plane of the soul, they are already true of me. I choose them out of a fidelity to self, not an aspiration toward an idealized self.

When asked to give a commencement address to a room of Spelman College graduates, the Reverend Howard Thurman spoke not of changing the world, but of listening to one's inner life. He said:

> There is in you something that waits and listens for the sound of the genuine in yourself and sometimes there is so much traffic going on in your minds, so many different kinds of signals, so many vast impulses floating through your organism that go back thousands of generations, long before you were even a thought in the mind of creation, and you are buffeted by these, and in the midst of all of this you have got to find out what your name is. Who are you?

You know the ache of hiding, of pretending to believe something, of words in conflict with the spirit. It does something to the soul—not in time but immediately and every time—when by choice or bondage or shame we are dragged out of ourselves into a miraged self. That journey erodes the marrow of the soul. The miraged self has no concern for the sound of the genuine in you, for the body, for the mind. It will not breathe for you. Do not be deceived; it does not want you hidden, it wants you dead. It is not dress-up; it is suffocation—a murderous exile. To survive it, we must gain a certain loyalty to our selfhood. We must free the part of ourselves that seeks to protect the self.

I've accepted that the whole of my life will be a pilgrimage toward the sound of the genuine in me. This may sound troubling to those who've been conditioned to believe that our journey is to God and God alone, but I say the two paths are one. My journey to the truth of God cannot be parsed from my journey to the truth of who I am. A fidelity to the true self is a fidelity to truth. I won't apologize for this.

If you want to decipher who you are, it's good to begin with the question of what stories have been told about you. Do this not because they are true but because they will help you locate the mirages and their origins. They will help you rend mask from flesh. They may also help you grab hold of something real.

Howard Thurman went on, "Now if I hear the sound of the genuine in me, and if you hear the sound of the genuine in you, it is possible for me to go down in me and come up in you. So that when I look at myself through your eyes having made that pilgrimage, I see in me what you see in me and the wall that separates and divides will disappear." This is his assurance that our calling into self need not be solitary. Nor is it only for the healing and protection of me. Just as outer voices can lead you away from the well of your own selfhood, they also have the capacity to usher you into new depths of it. And if practiced right, your calling into selfhood may enhance the sound of self in someone else.

. . .

My father can talk to a wall and convince it to crumble or stand three feet taller. He has three necks for each of his three voices, but they are all his own. He can talk to anyone and make them feel heard. He said white people call it the gift of gab. I call it a man at work. He might as well've been putting on a cape when he, smelling of cologne and Vitapointe, let his ankle-length trench coat float onto his shoulders and tapped out the door in his polished loafers. He was born to hustle, but most days I just wished he'd sit down and have a rest.

He says all he needed was a D in English to graduate from high school, and he got an F. That is, until he went to Mr. Lute and talked his way to freedom. I ask him how he did it. He says, *You think I told that man the truth?* Which was that he'd been working to help his single mom, that he was tired and distracted. *Hell no, I appealed to his vanity.* My father went on and on to him about how he was so grateful for a teacher who didn't give up on *the underdogs.* He told him he *wouldn't have made it this far without him,* that he was sorry. And it turns out the only thing that ran deeper than Mr. Lute's villainy was his desire to be a hero. He gave my father a D. At graduation, my father shook every teacher's hand but his. He didn't owe him a thing.

As a child, his first job was delivering groceries for twenty-five-cent tips. In middle school, on snow days, as the other kids were coiling back into sheets in celebration, he grabbed a shovel and started knocking on doors. In the summers, you could find him on his hands and knees cutting the perimeter of lawns with shears for his Uncle Jack, who was very particular about his yard business but paid a child more than minimum wage. In high school, he swept and scrubbed a dry-cleaning factory in the evenings for a man named Romeo. But in the mornings, you could find him first thing rolling joints thin as pins with Corey. They called them penitentiary joints—there was weed in there, but barely. Not enough to get anyone free.

Or maybe not enough to get anyone caught. My father and Corey would walk to school early and be waiting with their wares when the buses rolled in every day.

When people talk about calling as work, maybe they see a man in pleated pants and loafers. All I see is a boy turning thirty dollars into sixty dollars by first period.

Do you know Bezalel and Oholiab? God chose them to essentially build a movable temple in the wilderness: the Tabernacle. He gave them all kinds of knowledge and artistry so they could work with gold and silver and bronze. He gave them the skills to set stones and work in wood. I wonder if God took one look at my father and poured out charm all over him, tucked it into every fold, let it bubble up in every wound like peroxide. Maybe my father was given what he needed to make it.

Like many who don't have the socioeconomic privilege of really choosing their occupation, my father's calling to work (read: hustle) was not about what he would do; it was about how he would do it, and by what means of selfhood. He says he wanted to be an attorney. But underneath this, he desires a safety and security for others that he did not sense as a child. He's always been a wooer, but deeper still, he is a seer of people. He sees people in such a manner that they crave nearness to him. While he wanted to be an attorney, he never expected to be. He found his own way to live into these callings in him.

It can be difficult for me now to belong to rooms where people's chief idea of discerning their calling is deciding what job they'll choose. I've spent the past eight years working in Christian spaces within academia, often among people whose primary sense of calling is whether they were meant to be an engineer or a physicist. Defensively, I've found myself silently asking, Do you think you're the only ones God has "called"? What of the vast majority of the world, which does not have the liberty of making such a discernment? Do the little Black boys running the streets not have callings? And I have never heard a college student tell me they "feel called" to work at McDonald's. I remain very suspicious of this.

We cannot talk about work as calling without contending with the fact that there are those who have been denied choice, equity, and dignity in their work.

I had a boss who once suggested, as a part of a conversation on vocation with Cornell students, that we watch a short documentary about custodial staff at various universities. I wonder if he noticed the flash of hope in my face. Or was it desperation? There, strung up like a Black marionette between worlds—one of prestige and career fairs, and one of soft and single Black grammas with little boys who stopped their own dreaming—I was desperate for a synchrony that wouldn't tear me apart. I needed to know that it was, in fact, possible to honor the sacred in our work without creating spiritual hierarchies depending on the kind of labor being performed.

I do resonate with the theology that God is indeed in all things, including our work. To some, this is a novel idea. I play along in their company. But Black people in this country have never known it any other way. The concept of relegating God to church on Sunday is laughable to those whose very lives depend on a God who is with them as they're paying bills, getting pulled over by cops, and further back still, in fields of cotton. Every Black person I know would tell you what it took fancy theologians and philosophers years to articulate: God is in the streets.

How boring to spend the whole of my vocational energy trying to figure out if I am choosing the right work. It is of much greater interest to me to talk about how I'm going to do the work with integrity. How am I going to protect dignity as I work? And what truths are calling out to me as I work?

You may think we are called to holy things that involve praying on your knees and going to church, and maybe we are. But I haven't known God to regulate holiness. I think they injected it into every bit of everything. And I imagine they are very concerned with every element of life, including our work. And why wouldn't they be?

As a writer, I have to think that God cares deeply about the words on this page. If it's true that God made the whole world with the simple utterance of words, I think it's very possible they would allow for a sacred power in mine, and that this would allow me to commune with the divine in some mysterious way, and even that the craft and work of writing would have something to say about how the world hangs together, something to say about the divine. I could say the same about nearly every job or scheme. About math. Look at the equations in the leaves and the shells: God was the first mathematician. About art. Look at that sunset, the curve of your lips: God was the first artist. And not only does God care about washing floors with excellence, Christians tell the story of a God who got on his hands and knees one night and washed filth from feet. Excellence may be a part of calling, but work itself is a meeting place for the divine as we experience a God who labors alongside us.

Martin Luther King, Jr., said, "Even if it falls your lot to be a street sweeper, go on out and sweep streets like Michelangelo painted pictures; sweep streets like Handel and Beethoven composed music; sweep streets like Shakespeare wrote poetry; sweep streets so well that all the hosts of heaven and earth will pause to say, 'Here lived a great street sweeper who swept his job well.' " I wonder what God would say about my father's penitentiary joints. Maybe he would've grabbed his face and told him to walk away, to take all the holy hustle stirring within him and use it for goodness and beauty in the world. Or maybe he was standing there over my father's shoulder, telling him to quit playing and pack that thing right.

. . .

My gramma was in bed, but she knew she was still sleeping. In her dream, she was in her room, only she was not alone; she was surrounded by large figures. But she was calm as night when her Pa Paw curved over the bed and said in his worn out rasp, *Well, don't just sit dere, lil girl, you betta get on up and get a piece of paper—you gon want to write this down.* And she did. She sat there as he told her all secrets and stories, dark and light. He told her how her mother lost her eye—that he and her grandmother already had four children and knew one more would crush them all whole. He told her how he reached into that womb with a hook and tried to end it himself, but all he managed to take was an eye. How the whole house wept as her momma, whose existence began *in spite of,* came out bloodied and winking at the cosmos. The stories did not rest easy on the soul, but they were true, and Pa Paw told as many as he could.

She says they were all there, her family, alive and dead, and she could sense it. Even those she'd never met. All the aunties and cousins. Those who died too soon and who lived so long they became walking dust. Uncle Sonny's big ass was howling in the corner, skin black like the onyx stone in a crown of kings. He told her the same corny jokes he used to, his warmth and joy radiating into her and holding her upright from within. And she laughed and ached and they were together.

When she finally woke up, her insides had grown three sizes. She contained something true and she knew it. Turns out the story of her mother's lost eye actually happened. And now, whenever she doubts her dreaming, the things she contains, she remembers this night. The holy meeting of ancestors. Doubt cannot touch that room.

My gramma will tell you this story as plainly as she'll tell you her name or what time it is. I am not one given to belief, but I believe in her. It seems it is the one delicacy my mind will allow for itself. She says, *Nicole, now I'm gonna ask you this now*. And I sit up on the inside but lie back on the couch, sensing something heavy enter the space between us. She says, *Have you ever just known something? And you cannot say why or when you first knew it?* I had. *I'm not talking about a feeling; I'm talking about knowledge*. I knew.

Simone Weil said, "Man only escapes from the laws of this world in lightning flashes. Instants when everything stands still, instants of contemplation, of pure intuition, of mental void, of acceptance of the moral void. It is through such instants that he is capable of the supernatural." I don't yet know about the word *only*, but I think there is a truth in this. It makes me uncomfortable, because I've grown used to an existence that requires I prove every part of me. But I am learning a slow embrace of mystery, even those mysteries that reside in me.

I've never heard the voice of God, but I was sitting in a living room with my roommates and now-husband when I told them we were going to hit a deer soon, and they laughed and I laughed, because it is an absurd thing to say with such certainty. We called it anxiety, and maybe it was, but later that night, I was in the passenger seat when I said it again before I even knew I was saying it: *We're going to hit a deer.* And my husband laughed again, but for reasons we've never discussed, he still slowed. And then red-brown fur was falling like rain, and its quivering body lay twitching in the road, and he was saying, *It's okay. Are you okay? It's okay.* And apart from a dented-in front bumper and two trembling bodies, it was. That deer twitched back to life and leapt back over the guardrail like it was onstage, and I its director.

It does not, in fact, matter to me if it was coincidence or insight or the ancestors' whispers that told me to tell my husband to slow down that day. All I know is I'm glad as hell I said it. I don't need there to be anything special about it, but as one who believes that mystery swells the womb of every given moment, I've made a point never to preclude it.

. . .

Picture me now clasping your cheeks. I'm looking in your eyes, and maybe you're dreaming. I'm telling you, *Don't forget this: Nothing is truly ever ordinary.* I'm telling you, *Protect the truest things about you and it will become easier to hear the truth everyplace else.*

I'm still listening. My calling came on the chords of my father's voice and my gramma's dreaming. Hear it in the cadence of my words. I cannot now name the song, but when I hear the sound, I will recognize it.

FIVE

Body

She told me blood was coming. Sitting side by side on a floppy twin bed stripped down to its floral skin, I dug my eyes into our reflection in the dome of the black TV screen in the corner. It made us look big. She drew a diagram on the paper towel that I had just eaten pretzels off of. *You see there? That's where your eggs live.* She spoke as tender as your parents on the day they tell you Santa isn't real. I never believed in Santa and disliked my Aunt Jenny's tenderness now.

It took a lot to look down at the drawing, but I did. It was good as labyrinth to me, and I listened as together we went into that paper towel—winding in and out of ridges and paths until I found a shame that didn't belong to me. I learned of blood and babies while sitting on faded roses. And the thorns lifted from that polyester mattress and tried to bleed me out. Aunt Jenny rushed the softness of her own skin underneath mine to keep them from digging too deep. *And honey, there ain't nothing to be ashamed of.* She recognized the shadow creeping over my face. It was all she could do to try to push it back with hers. *No shame.*

I have often wondered if Mary, even with full knowledge and proclamation of the glory of her womb, felt shame for it. As her body changed and belly grew, did she question if it was worthy to hold the divine? Was she embarrassed of the stories her body contained? The weakness, the inflammation, the smell. Or did she see her flesh for what it was—holy? Weak, powerful, human, and holy.

For me, the story of God becoming body is only matched by God's submission to the body of a woman. That the creator of the cosmos would choose to rely on an embodied creation. To be grown, fed, delivered—God put faith in a body. In Mary's muscles and hormones, bowels and breasts. And when Christ's body is broken and blood shed, we should hold in mystery that first a woman's body was broken, her blood shed, in order to deliver the hope of the world into the world.

We are remarkably material beings. When we speak of bearing the image of God, I believe no small part of that is a physical bearing. You may have heard it said, "You don't have a soul. You are a soul. You have a body." I'm not sure exactly where this notion came from, but the sentiment survives. Many of us, in pursuit of the spiritual, become woefully neglectful of the physical. We concern ourselves with a doctrine of salvation that is oriented around one underlying hope: heaven. And our concepts of heaven are often disembodied—a spiritual goal to transcend the material world eternally. You've seen the bumper sticker, slapped crooked on that dusty sedan. It reads: *This place is not my home.*

I don't know much about heaven, but I have no reason to believe it won't be made right here. Those faded rose beds will spring up from their graves singing bloody hallelujahs. My gramma's muumuu will stretch and wrap around the belly of the world, cradling it till it stops crying and everything smells like Shalimar perfume. Who says I'm going anywhere but here?

Our tales of Christian escapism lead us to the place where the physical is damned and the immaterial is gloried. Where the only holy things are invisible. How could you expect me to believe this when I've met a God who drank from the breast of his creation?

I was in middle school when my great-aunt's husband died and we began going to church with her for a while so she didn't have to go alone. It was a Baptist church on a hill, made of hand-hewn logs and white faces. And it's where I first heard about a God who died on a cross. It was a Good Friday service, and the pastor, a small man with hair slick like oil and veins that stained his flesh blue, was pacing the stage. He began gesticulating wildly, sweat collecting on his upper lip like a strand of tiny pearls that he sprayed out to the audience as he yelled. *And they DROVE the nails right here,* he said, digging his thumb and pointer fingers into his wrist. *And they took the nest of thorns and RAMMED it on his scalp.* And he hammered his own skull with his fist. My sister grabs my knee. *This dude okay?* And my father glares a warning down at us, but we can tell he is trying not to crack up. *This is what JEEZUS gave for you,* the blue man cries. I flinch, and my sister squeezes my knee tighter. *He gave his BLOOD. What will you give? Is he worth your LIFE? Will you give your life to him today?* And he beats against his chest like a locked door.

After the service, our parents went to eat bagels and act somber with my great-aunt and the other adults, and I curled up in my sister's shadow as she rotated around the stations of the cross with the other kids. She brought a vinegar-soaked sponge to my mouth and whispered, *Pretend*. And we giggled as the other kids winced and went back for more. As a finale, they made us write down our deepest loves and throw them into a fire in the parking lot. *Jesus wants it all. Will you give your life for him?* My sister took a slip and wrote for both of us: *We're too young to die*. And then, almost as an afterthought: *Sorry*. We threw it in the flame.

In hindsight, this was my first encounter with a spirituality that demanded my death far more often than it ever advocated for my life. It was as if because God endured bodily violence, it became a requirement for the rest of us. That we should sacrifice our bodies, knowing that eternal salvation awaited our souls. This was the eerie heartbeat of this small log cabin church: Your body is expendable.

And it's not only them. I think whiteness knows that the more detached I am from my body, the easier that body will be to colonize and use toward whiteness's own ends. It desires that my mind be fixed firmly on an immaterial realm, that I become numb to any present and material injustices. It is this belief system that indoctrinates us to sneer at social justice but bow to evangelism. After all, evangelism has the ability to exercise the same muscles as colonization—telling someone what to think and be. It can be a form of ownership in the name of heaven. All our charades of honoring the invisible things at the expense of the material serve to obscure the very material injustices by which Black people have been historically excluded.

That is not to say I disbelieve in an unseen spiritual realm. On the contrary, I believe that the spiritual realm is so enmeshed with the physical that it is imperceptible. I believe in the mysterious nearness of my ancestors, but I believe they are located at the site of my own blood and bone.

The chasm between the spiritual and the physical is no greater than that between a thought and a word. They cannot be disconnected. And it is difficult to tell where one ends and the other begins, perhaps because there is no such place.

We were never meant to dismember our selfhoods. My face is my soul is my blood is my glory. When we neglect the physical, it inevitably suffocates the image of a God who ate, slept, cried, bled, grew, and healed. And whether or not the origin of that neglect is hatred, it will indeed end in hatred.

I want a faith that loves the whole of me. And if I make it to the table of God, I hope it has cornbread stuffing and comfortable chairs. I mean no offense to the desert mothers and fathers eating locusts and honey and itching with camel hair, but I hope God knows how my cousin's baked mac and cheese tastes. I hope he puts ham hocks in his greens and feels no shame.

. . .

In third grade, when my gramma still ran around the schoolyard like delight was hers to have, her teacher pulled her aside and handed her a note for home with a look. *That* look. If the teacher grimaced or growled, I cannot say, but she found a way to make her disgust known as she dug her eyes into my gramma's chest. She tucked the note under her backpack strap and through the hole in her sweater, where its message punctured the skin and rested inside her.

After reading it, the woman who was not my gramma's mother sighed once, curled it up tight, and then sent it back through that same hole, where it lives to this day, right under her flesh: *Phyllis cannot run around the schoolyard without a bra. Body changing.* And what hatred the woman who was not her mother felt for my gramma was only magnified by the fact that she had to now spend money on a bra for an eight-year-old.

When shame enters us, it tends to make its home in our bodies. My gramma's body became a new kind of burden. In a room of children, the lone body that required bondage changed the way she moved. She stopped running at recess. *From then on, I only slouched. I was buried within myself.* By that age, she had known she was despised for her Blackness, but this new shame no one had prepared her for. And it began to occur to her that the things that had begun happening *to* her body were her fault. *What I hafta do to be left alone?* she wondered. *What'd I do to be found in the first place?* To this day, she doesn't look up in the mirror over the bathroom sink. Some days, she'll look down and think, *Whose arm is this?*

I, too, know the haunting of body become spectacle. When Gerald Wiand leaned in close with a confused expression and told me I looked like *a pug dog, no offense*, I Googled "pug dog" at free time and by recess had turned against my own face. When your body becomes something consumed or rejected, it is a rejection not just of body but also of soul.

Gerald was there three years later when I, the lone Black body in the room, was asked to read a Maya Angelou poem at the front of the class by a teacher who used to call me by another Black girl's name. And he was there eight years after that when my face was plastered on the backs of thousands of program booklets at the conference of a white-dominated Christian organization. My body as spectacle, as token, has become very familiar to me. There is a feverish cannibalism for Black bodies. I won't be blamed for what I did to survive it.

. . .

Trauma changes the body. Some research suggests it leaves its mark on our genes, a mark that can be inherited from generation to generation. This transference does not altogether surprise me, as I am among those who believe that we are made of our histories, that no part of me is untouched by the glories and traumas that gave birth to me. But a certain helplessness comes over me when I truly consider that I might be affected not only by my present pain but also by the agony of my ancestors. Though I would never wish away my connection to those who endured and resisted violence and exclusion, I have to contend with what their stories are doing to my body. And I tremble to think what parts of my storied blood will flow through the bodies of any children I have.

But before it changes the bodies of my children, the trauma of this world will change the body of me. Dutch psychiatrist Bessel van der Kolk writes:

> Traumatized people chronically feel unsafe inside their bodies: The past is alive in the form of gnawing interior discomfort. Their bodies are constantly bombarded by

> visceral warning signs, and, in an attempt to control these processes, they often become expert at ignoring their gut feelings and in numbing awareness of what is played out inside. They learn to hide from their selves.

When people speak of dissociation, they speak like it's a door you walk through and can walk back out of once you've learned you meant to go right and not left. It's more like falling asleep and realizing you're dreaming but being unable to wake up. You can never really see yourself in a dream. You live, but with senses numbed and faces blurred. To wake up requires more than an awareness that you have fallen asleep. You are roused to consciousness by will, mystery, and the long passage of the night.

If you feel unsafe or rejected in your body for long enough, after a while it becomes understandable that you might be inclined to forsake it. I remember when I first told my white-skinned husband that I often forgot to eat until the sun started setting and I realized night was coming. For weeks, I thought about the look he gave me. It never occurred to him that a woman whose survival felt like it depended on being able to forget her body would find herself doing so without even trying.

Without healing and integration, we can begin to blame our bodies for this—turning against them as enemies distinct from ourselves. Who invited this nose and these lips to live here? You know those secret things you speak over your body when you're not looking? You weren't the first to speak them.

From Ta-Nehisi Coates:

> But all our phrasing—race relations, racial chasm, racial justice, racial profiling, white privilege, even white supremacy—serves to obscure that racism is a visceral experience, that it dislodges brains, blocks airways, rips muscle, extracts organs, cracks bones, breaks teeth. You must never look away from this. You must always remember that the sociology, the history, the economics, the graphs, the charts, the regressions all land, with great violence, upon the body.

What great violence has this flesh endured? What chills sail up my spine, and when? We cannot get free disembodied. There is no promised land without a tongue to taste the milk and honey. We may forsake the body in order to survive, but the truth is that we do so at our own peril.

Bessel van der Kolk also writes:

> Trauma victims cannot recover until they become familiar with and befriend the sensations in their bodies. Being frightened means that you live in a body that is always on guard. . . . People need to become aware of their sensations and the way that their bodies interact with the world around them. Physical self-awareness is the first step in releasing the tyranny of the past.

In a world desperate to make an enemy of my body, how will I befriend it? Will I put my faith in it—that the gloried physical will resurrect the power, pleasure, protection, and presence I was meant for?

. . .

She put the needle in my arm and said it wouldn't take long. I was living in Ithaca and had been sick for a year before a neurologist ordered an MRI. I felt the warmth from the dye in my veins immediately.

I said, *My ears are burning*. She said, *Strange—never heard of that*. My nose started to feel like someone was forcing cotton through the passages. I said, *My nose*. She said, *I'll be right in the next room*. I said, *My throat*, and it was collapsing. My chest began to swell. *I can't breathe*. She said, *Are you feeling anxious?* I said, *I can't breathe*. She said, *Do you have anxiety?* I shook my head no, feeling my neck constrict like a closed fist. I parted my lips once more—the calmness in my voice could not match the terror of the truth, which was: *Listen, please. In about sixty seconds, I will not be able to breathe. I do not think I will be able to speak. Please get a doctor now, please*. I blacked out.

Tell my father that on the door of death, I still had the mind to say please.

When I was roused the first time, a man with glasses like goggles was flashing a light into my eyes, and they were speeding me on a metal coffin down the hospital corridor. A half dozen of my escorts toppled into a brightly lit room. They asked me my name as something sharp pierced my flesh. My thigh lit up with epinephrine and my whole body quaked. And I knew I was dying.

We know our bodies. When I went into anaphylactic shock during that MRI, I never once wondered what was happening;

I only wondered if I could get someone to believe me in time. We know our bodies. Some more than others, but each of us knows.

I was twenty-six when I became sick, and I knew a disease had crept into me. How does one articulate that one just knows—that this shoulder is not the shoulder I know, that these hands move but not in the way they learned to? It took a long time to convince someone that I knew my body.

I was twenty-seven, and my husband had begun secretly tying my shoes for me and feeding me my own dinner, and we weren't receiving any concrete answers. First an orthopedist, then neurologist, then rheumatologist, immunologist, speech and swallow therapy, neuro-optometrist, and back to the neurologist. They stuck needles in me and sent shocks through my nerves. They lathered paste on a ham sandwich and watched it travel down my throat. They stole fluid from my spine while I lay in the fetal position.

After dozens of hospitals and hundreds of appointments, I've learned that this world has no commitments to my body. No one will try to understand it more than I will. I learned the necessity not only of listening to your own body but also of fighting for it. When the burning and twitching came, I learned man will never sit still long enough to watch for them. And when the rashes came, I learned man will never search my skin for as long as I need him to. We are poorly attuned to one another's bodies. It is a latent evil.

To know your own body is a spiritual care and protection. To know the body of another is a spiritual union and conciliation. We must become so acquainted with the physical good that when evil, affliction, sickness, and pain come, we can name them with the urgency they demand. These hands may move, but not the way *my* hands move. There are times when this sacred fidelity to self—fully embodied soul-self—may keep us from death itself.

The disease alienated me from my body before it alienated me from others. I slept flat on my back for a whole year. I promise you I never rolled over, not once. Terrified of my body, of its pain, I would lie in bed all day, reading and writing and watching documentaries that enhanced my intellectual ego. If I could not have my body, I thought, at least I would have my mind. I do not hold this against myself, but I do regret the love I stole from my body when it so desperately needed it. When our bodies feel small to us, we do what we can to expand our dignity elsewhere.

I'm learning to befriend my body again. It does not always move the way I want it to, but I have made a commitment that if it ceases to move at all, if I lose all control and agency, if my hands go numb in the night and never wake again, even still I will not forsake my body.

To be people capable of extending welcome to the body, even those bodies the world discards and demeans, is to be people of profound liberation. By this we will know our faith: We will stay whole.

. . .

This is my body. Broken. This is my blood. Drained. Eat. Drink. Do this in remembrance of me.

It is queer and beautiful that some of us belong to a God who tells us to consume his body and blood in remembrance. What do the body and blood have to do with memory? How do they connect us to the story of liberation? It means something that the Eucharist, this lasting ritual of the presence and memory of God, is a physical nourishment as much as it is spiritual. I once went to a church that gave everyone a whole slice of bread and they actually buttered it. It felt wrong, but they had something so right. I love that we don't just bow to the bread, we eat it—the body of God entering our bodies. And I think God's supposed to taste good.

That we have managed to regurgitate a Christian spirituality that is anything less than bodily glory, agony, healing, and restoration is our tragedy. I don't think it an accident that we are made to remember God through an act that nourishes us in our own bodies. I've heard much of bodily sacrifice, of taking up a cross, of dying and dying again. But I need to hear of resurrection—of the bodily love of receiving the Eucharist.

You want to tell me to love God? Ask me when I've last eaten. Come now, you want me to tell you a prayer? You'll find it in the blood beating from heart to head to toe and home again.

Don't ask me of salvation. Listen to the hum of my chest as I now fall asleep. I cannot see the face of God by rejecting my own.

SIX

Belonging

Long, long ago, when all the earth was still as silence, the moon got all choked up on the beauty of the stars. She coughed and then wind was born. The wind rushed out with such a force she didn't even know where she came from at all. She started roaming and searching, darting through trees and trying to wrap herself around anything she could find. No matter what she did, it was as if she was invisible. She wanted to rest in something, but no place would have her. Whenever she became really desperate, she would rend herself into cold and hot air and collide with herself. This, of course, made a tornado of her. So she would thrash through places with an ugliness, picking everything up and forcing it to be held by her, even if just for a little while.

Until one day, God was in the garden making something like their own image, and they saw her, and their heart went out to her. And so God inhaled a little bit of her and blew it right into the breast of the image. The wind went on searching and remains very lonely to this day—only every once in a while, when she passes by a human or caresses a cheek on a summer day, the wind God put in you and me will stir and recognize herself for a moment. And those tiny moments of being seen, of being felt, collect like a hope in her, carrying her through her loneliness to this day.

We were made for belonging. I don't need a verse in Genesis to tell me that it is not good for one to be alone. Not always.

I do join the scores of others who have said that, in more ways than one, the flourishing of a healthy community lies in the ability of its parts to be solitary. Our pining for belonging can do frenetic things to the soul. We can become so desperate for connection that we make havoc from all the hungry parts of ourselves. It makes us restless. It can make us consume others instead of embrace them. Maybe we habitually ignore the boundaries of a friend because we fear absence will end in abandonment. Or we make unhealthy demands of relationships to satisfy our own insecurities, desperate for affirmation. Solitude can be a profound teacher. It can teach us how to hold ourselves—how to affirm ourselves and listen. How much is the sound of your own voice worth?

And yet, we were made for belonging. Maybe you've heard it said that you need to learn how to be alone before you can be with someone. I say you have to learn how to be with and a part of something in order to know how to be alone. I think it is only out of a deep anchoring in community that one can ever be free to explore the solitary.

When I write *community,* I mean to say any group of people that is committed to being a collective. I currently live in a small, predominantly white lake town. So when I'm at the farmer's market and I look up and see another brown-skinned face staring back at me, a mystery stretches out between us. We nod and know that the wind in us has stirred—that we have known enough of the same things to feel like we are made of the same thing. With one look, we commune. And we breathe. We remember our Blackness holds us together, and we are held.

A community can mean a household, a local body, a shared identity that stretches across the globe. But it also can mean a group that knows your name, people who know you and know about the ugly parts of you and stay.

I was in my midtwenties and living in West Philly in a row-home so narrow you had to dance with each other just to pass in the hallway. I called it the House of No Hiding, which is to say, I was looking to remain hidden. There were three of us. We used to joke that we looked like a commercial trying to meet a diversity quota: Black, white, and Taiwanese American. We were each so distinct it'd be easy to make caricatures out of us. The quirky one, the sophisticated one, the loner. We're at this Pakistani restaurant down the street, bowing over naan like it's manna, when the two others make their confession. *We didn't know if you hated us.* And I'm laughing with them but I don't know at what. Esther puckers her mouth out and bobbles her head with her eyes closed. *How we supposed to know? We don't know. You just leave.*

At this particular table, I was the loner. For a year, every day I'd come home and go straight to my room and close the door. Schug and Esther would be rustling around in the kitchen together, trading the secrets and stories that made up their days. I wish I could tell you that it never occurred to me that this simple act of habitual distance had any effect on them. The truth is, I knew. But scared even now to come out of hiding, I feign ignorance, hoping it will protect me from needing to articulate why this daily retreat felt so necessary to me.

I stop chewing and let the naan rest on my tongue, my eyes swaying between them as they carefully explain what it was like to be friends with a Cole who was always nowhere. We keep laughing, and I ask what changed. But I am actually wondering why two people would go to such great lengths to preserve friendship with someone they aren't sure wants them back. And almost as if I have wondered it aloud, Schug shoves me gently with her shoulder and says, *We just know you. You aren't us, and maybe we need that in you.* Esther flutters her eyelashes and coos theatrically, *Better togetherrrr.*

Dietrich Bonhoeffer writes, "In a Christian community everything depends upon whether each individual is an indispensable link in a chain. Only when even the smallest link is securely interlocked is the chain unbreakable. A community which allows unemployed members to exist within it will perish." When he uses the word "unemployed," I don't believe Bonhoeffer is talking about employment in the economic sense but rather as a fostering of purpose. He meant that each part of a community would have agency to affect the whole, in whatever way that may be—that the community's survival would depend on each link. I have a friend who calls this mutuality, the truth that says, *We don't just welcome you or accept you; we need you. We are insufficient without you.* One part's absence renders the whole impoverished in some way, even if the whole didn't previously apprehend it. In mutuality, belonging is both a gift received and a gift given. There is comfort in being welcomed, but there is dignity in knowing that your arrival just shifted a group toward deeper wholeness.

People talk about God as three distinct people in one. If this is true, it means the whole cosmos is predicated on a diverse and holy community. And if we bear the image of God, that means we bear the image of a multitude. And that to bear the image of God in its fullness, we need each other. Maybe every culture, every household, every community bears that image in a unique way.

. . .

I walked into that room of mirrors trembling. My three-dollar tights were scared like me, squirming their way up my back, using my butt as a hiding place. My head throbbed from the polished bun my father had just slicked my wild hair into. I looked up: Everyone was beaming, and everyone was white.

A thin blond woman with toes that looked like swollen baby carrots descended to look me in the eye and said, *Why don't you go take a place?* as she pointed to the barre. I was seven and was not one to invite my presence into anyone's space, so I walked past about twenty other little girls and made my way to the farthest end of the barre. I was nearly hanging off.

When the music started, I began following what I could see. I was at the very back of the line, and everyone was looking forward, so I was free to move like I was made to. Until we relevéd and switched sides, and I was laid bare. The teacher shimmied up to my end of the barre, now the front, and gave me a wink. I glanced and caught a look in the mirror, and that's when I saw it. I looked down at my little black ballet shoes and my eyes darted down the line, and would you believe that every little girl in that line was pointing the toes of pink ballet shoes? In this moment, I both hated them and wanted to be them. I wanted to disappear. I felt betrayed, but I wasn't sure by whom. No matter the other girls were also *all white;* I think my brain needed to make it about the shoes. I spent all night in front of those mirrors, and all I could see was black.

On the car ride home, I begged my stepmom to buy me pink ballet shoes. Never mind that we couldn't even afford the classes themselves. She told me that the teacher said mine were just fine. But she must've felt something in my voice or my silence, because the next day when she picked us up from school, she said, *Look in the box,* with a kind of mischief on her face. I did. There lay pink, and it felt like salvation.

It was not. It took years for me to feel any kind of belonging. I was dead silent in class. But I learned to mimic the teacher's body with such precision. I think I thought this mimicry would lead to welcome. But I got good. And the whispers started. I watched their faces smirk at one another behind my back in the mirror. It wasn't everyone, but it was enough that when my classmates all began taking their breaks in the back waiting room, I would sit in the front room alone, pretending not to notice.

Exclusion operates by the same rule of mutuality as welcome, for it harms both the excluded and the excluder. If you are the hands of exclusion for long enough, you learn acceptance only at the hands of someone else's exile. You learn belonging as competition, not restoration. It is also a kind of restlessness, for the energy you expend forbidding others to walk through the door of community is only matched by the energy you expend competing to stay inside yourself. This is maybe more dangerous; no one ever perceives the doorkeeper as needing an invitation themselves.

Exclusion compounds any shame that already dwells in the body. And it was shame that pulsed in me when I told my stepmom that I chose to room with people I didn't know for our fifth-grade end-of-year trip so that my friends could room with each other and no one felt left out. She said she was proud of me. Only no one asked me to be in their room on that trip. My teacher held back three of us after class one day and let us know that since none of us had been chosen, we would all be together. Belonging by default isn't the worst thing, but there is something to being chosen that is uniquely healing. It communicates to the soul that one is desired not passively but with an active longing. A longing that has moved someone to do something about it. No one was moved for me. In a cruel act of fate, on day two of that trip, I got chicken pox from Joshua Ward and ended up alone in a room with a chaperone. No one was allowed to touch me, and all of the kids would scurry away in terror, thinking that proximity to me and my bumps meant certain death.

I wonder if God feels as alienated from us as we do from him. Sometimes, it cracks me up to think of the stories that describe Christ just boldly inviting himself over to people's houses for dinner. Roaming around telling people to stop everything and follow him. Multiplying food, but making everyone sit down in groups to eat it. He knew how to make his own belonging. Do we?

. . .

My gramma was in college coming home from church one day, and one of the choir guys asked if she needed a ride home. *He was the giant on campus,* she says. *Everybody liked him.* She doesn't even remember saying yes, but they were outside her apartment when he told her how much he wanted to live off campus. He told her he was looking for a place and he'd sure like to come inside and see for himself. And she doesn't remember saying yes, but he did. And he didn't give a damn about the kitchen size, or the water pressure, or the noise from across the street. Two steps inside the door, he was all over her. He just kept touching her like he owned the place and she came with it. At first, she just tried to dip and dodge politely, let him down but let him down easy. But he wouldn't go down easy. His hands gripped tighter. His eyes looked dead. What saved her would also be the moment that shattered her.

Her best friend started knocking on the door, and *she needed something so she wasn't going nowhere.* My gramma slid out of the man's grip for long enough to fling wide the door. And still unsure of what to say, she said the first thing that came to mind. *Please. Come in.* But this girl, who had grown up with her—who had known every secret including the despair behind my gramma's smile—this girl sees my gramma's blouse undone and her hair disheveled, and gives her one disgusted and complicated look and walks away.

The next day, even the trees were whispering about her. My gramma tried to tell her friend. She tried to explain how badly she needed her to come inside that day. But the girl who in the end was not a friend at all just looked her up and down once and said, *I didn't want to interrupt anything.*

My gramma crumbled.

And that was the last best friend I ever allowed myself to have.

If you go without belonging for long enough, if you've known the sting of betrayal, you can end up manufacturing an identity from your alienation. To protect yourself from the reminder and risk of exclusion, you begin initiating distance on your own, calling yourself "loner" or "independent." This becomes a form of lived escapism as you run from the belief that you will be rejected again or that you cannot trust again. But a life lived with trust only in the self is exhausting. It is not freedom; it is a yoke that falls helplessly and incessantly on you.

Some will contrive delusions of superiority to community itself. You tell yourself that no one can or will ever understand you or your complexities. You make bravado out of your loneliness. It is one way to numb the pain of the wound. You elevate yourself above community, looking down at it as frivolous or needy or less enlightened—this is in denial of your own needs, of course.

Both of these responses must be dismantled delicately, for underneath is the wound of not being embraced or known or cared for well by those whom you have longed to know and care for you.

. . .

My father encountered the social conditions of the school bus far too late in life. In Manhattan, they walked or took the city bus, so when he moved to Pittsburgh, he knew nothing of the grim habitat of adolescent angst and dominion that made up this strange yellow-encased society. He was unprepared. Back then, Pittsburgh was Black and white, and kids didn't know how to place his honey skin and Bronx accent. He sat alone and told himself he wasn't afraid.

He was small, scrawny, and mixed, and for it all he endured precisely three days of teasing. But on the third day, a meteor fell from the sky and stopped the bus dead in its tracks. And the glowing rock climbed on the bus and looked him right in the eyes, and everyone seemed to know the rock and wanted to be chosen by it, and they couldn't stop staring. And before anyone could ever say another word about my father's curly hair or the way he talked, the rock rolled onto the seat next to him and said, *I'm Corey.*

My father soon learned that no one starts shit with meteors, and he also learned that he was one of the few people who knew how to touch him and not get burned. And Corey soon learned that this small creature next to him had a magic tongue and limbs that could cast spells over any kind of person. A new gravity enshrouded them both, a cosmic tethering that would not easily be overcome.

At the intersection of belonging and choice, you'll often find friendship. It is that rare bond in which attachment feels so much like a risk because its origin lies in the bond itself. In households, the bond is situated in the home. Neighbors create communities bonded by proximity—block parties and borrowing sugar. Families have the bond of lineage—the stories that have formed you, your great-grandma's cornbread recipe. Friendship can, of course, be found in the home, neighborhood, or blood, but it doesn't necessarily begin there. It is two or more disparate parts being compelled toward one another by interest, circumstance, or even loneliness. We feel a distinct longing for this out of our longing to be chosen. That's not to say that bonds of choice are necessarily more important, but perhaps, just like bonds of fate or location, they nourish a particular part of the soul. Each day Corey chose my father and my father chose him, they were reminded they were wanted and worth wanting.

I think the terror of bonds of friendship is that just as they can be chosen, they can be unchosen. You might say this of all bonds, but in friendship the risk is perhaps felt more acutely. I'm convinced that in most bonds it is not conflict we fear; it is abandonment after conflict. We fear it because we know something is at risk. For this reason, we can become cruelest to those we know will stay. And we resort to flattery or appeasement for those we are uncertain will do so.

This can lead us to drink from shallow waters. Durable friendship is a bond that is able to endure both truth-telling and conflict. Bonds without these things become brittle. When your standing is always at stake in the group, it fosters assimilation and competition. A room full of mirrors and a tiny girl in black ballet shoes willing to sacrifice herself, her very skin, to belong. In spaces such as this, people will do and say what they otherwise would not if their standing felt sure.

But if you took this notion to the extreme, you would observe something interesting: There is a point at which the uncertainty becomes so great that the brittle bond is actually strengthened. On the other side of that line, you will find not community, but cult—where a sense of deep alienation meets the poisoned possibility of belonging through the death of selfhood. Cults may appear to exercise community, but it is a community that does not stand for each of its members. Cults stand only on behalf of a single member. And it is never reciprocal.

At the opposite end of the spectrum from cults, you find communities of true solidarity. Solidarity is a group that stands together, and would do so for even its weakest member. It is that community which resists the intoxicating lie of individualism—we live for ourselves and by ourselves. Solidarity dismisses self-preservation in favor of a new way—to sense the injustice, need, or glory of any one part as the unflinching responsibility of the collective.

My father said it didn't take long for people to understand that if they messed with Corey, they messed with him, and vice versa. The two of them stood as if they had only one set of legs to stand on. If one needed protection, they both did. If one wasn't safe, neither was. They shared everything. Corey came from more money, so he would sneak my father clothes and shoes so he didn't feel less than anyone. There were times Corey would want to pop off and fight this or that clique, and my father would try to get him to just walk away. He'd tell Corey he was out, but he never left. Their danger, their survival, their welfare, their joy—it was always going to be one. *We didn't need to say we'd die for each other,* he says. *But to this day, I'd bet my life on it.*

Jesus said there's no greater love than someone dying for their friend. I think of my father, and Corey, and the crew they ran the streets with—their love is no less sacred.

. . .

I was staring at my father in the mirror one day when it occurred to me he didn't look like his reflection. I said, *Do you think that is your face?* He looked at me like I was setting up a joke. I wasn't. With the mirror reversing his image, it was clear that his eyes weren't in the right place. It looked like someone was trying to re-create him, but they couldn't line up his lips right, and everything got thrown off a hair. *That's not your face.* It was the first time it occurred to me that we will never really see our own faces. We can see a mirror, and it's doing its best—but that is not your face, just an image of it, reversed and distorted. I remember thinking how much more handsome my father was in real life. I wanted to tell him but couldn't find the words. So I just grabbed him and stared.

We need other people to see our own faces—to bear witness to their beauty and truth. God has made it so that I can never truly know myself apart from another person. I cannot trust myself to describe the curve of my nose because I've never seen it. I want someone to bear witness to my face, that we could behold the image of God in one another and believe it on one another's behalf.

Audre Lorde said, "Without community there is no liberation." There is no promised land without a multitude. You think you can get there alone, and maybe by some rare chance you do. But what will become of the promise when it is collapsed by loneliness? Who is going to drink all that milk and honey with you? Look down in the cool, running stream. You cannot see yourself.

SEVEN

Fear

They are getting ready to fight the Manchester crew, each squad posted up talking shit like sonnets. A choir of teenage Black boys.

> *Man, fuck you, nigga, you weak as hell, yo.*
> *Man, you ain't shit, fuck outta here or step.*

The concrete stretches out underneath them like a stage, and they're all trembling—they got coal in their throats, and their hearts are pressing up against their chests trying to touch each other from the inside out. They pull their upper lips to meet a nostril of their choice, and they let their elbows dance higher than their pointed fingers. And they're all trembling and saying things they know to say as they listen for a cue that only they can perceive. There! But just when they start throwing hands, my father hears a crack, and Harry, not six feet away from him. Harry forgets his line and just says, *Ow, they burnt me*. Only it wasn't a crack but a gunshot, and it wasn't a burn but a hole in Harry's side. And my father trembles. Harry's blood seeps into the concrete until it starts to whistle, and everyone exits in different directions. They spread out to the ends of the earth, lips still pulled to keep them from quivering.

I guess we were afraid, my father says now with a shrug. A pause, and then the truth: *We were scared as hell. That shit was heavy. I guess that's why it's easier when you're not alone. You don't get less scared, but it's harder to tell.*

When we were young and still learning, they gave us facial expressions on a chart to identify the different emotions, and it occurs to me now that the chart's face for fear was not any fear I've ever seen. That cartoon face was shock, surprise maybe, but who can truly draw a portrait of fear?

For something at the root of so much of human behavior, it is rare that we ever truly behold another person's fear. So many of us express our fear in ways that only serve to mask it. In conflict, we may see anger or hate or apathy, but it is much more difficult to perceive fear in a person. It's even more difficult to name it. Yet fear stalks so much of our words and actions and even loves.

I'm told the most frequent command from God in the Bible is *Do not fear.* Some have interpreted this as an indictment on those who are afraid, as if to say fear signifies a less robust faith. This offends me. God is not criticizing us for being afraid in a world haunted by so many terrors and traumas. I hear *Don't be afraid* and hope that it is not a command not to fear but rather the nurturing voice of a God drawing near to our trembling. I hear those words and imagine God in all tenderness cradling her creation against her breast.

Perhaps it is not the indictment of God we are sensing but our own souls turned against themselves. I wouldn't dare criticize Christ in the garden—sweating, crying, pleading for God to let the cup pass from him. This is a Christ who knew fear deeply. And if God himself has been afraid, I have to believe he is tender with our own fear.

I'm scared of everything, I really am. I once hung trembling from a rock wall for nearly an hour at a rib cook-off. Until my sister made the worker call my father (who, alongside my stepmom, was one of the volunteers in charge of the whole thing) on his walkie-talkie. And next thing you know, my father was suspended in a harness next to me, whispering, *Reach, stand, reach, stand,* while the crowd chanted for me below. This is Arthur family lore. We tell it knowing I am still more scared than brave. I didn't conquer a fear, I rose to meet it. This is rare in me.

I'm afraid often enough that I've learned the different faces of fear. There is a fear that is attached to the past. Maybe you once encountered some terror that made such an incision that the mere memory of it can drag you back into the fear. Traumas and triggers. There is a present fear—a crack and a hole in Harry's side. This is a situation unfolding in the present, or at least in the moments following the present. This kind of fear is often wrapped up in pain or survival. Something immediate is at stake. You aren't waiting for the horror, it is here. There is nothing left to wonder but how much the horror will take from you.

Then there are those things we call "fears" themselves—

concerns of future abandonment, embarrassment, death, or loss. I think this is the form most hidden from ourselves. This is because fears tend to hide behind one another. Ask fifty people what they are afraid of and see how many say heights or spiders and how few have the presence of self to say they are afraid of abandonment or a deteriorating mind. I yell at my husband to *get out,* not because I want him to leave but because I am terrified that he will. I am not afraid of snakes; I'm afraid of pain, of immobilization or death. Telling the deepest truth of the fear requires thorough acquaintance with our own stories and interior lives, and it can so easily bleed into this next form of fear, a fear that endures past particular situations and can very nearly transcend time: anxiety.

Fear becomes anxiety when it makes its home in you. Its chief attachment is not memory or villain or situation or future; its chief attachment and subject is you. This strange and imprecise fear can torment the body and enshroud all other fear experiences.

As an antagonist, fear can disrupt the most sacred patterns of rest and restoration. Fear reminds us that we are not in control, that there is far more in life that is inevitable than preventable. In response, we grasp and cling to what control we have. When the coronavirus pandemic began and the stay-at-home orders were announced, it would have been reasonable to expect a season of rest, of a certain slowness. Instead, we observed the opposite; most of the people I know actually began to work *more*. Anxiety increased. And in the wake of global fear, we constructed illusions of safety and control. The more we habitualize using our fear to grasp at control, the more disrupted our rhythms of rest become.

Whenever my friend's ma was fed up, she used to mumble, *I might be limpin through the valley of the shadow of death . . .* What I skipped over in the psalm she was referencing time and time again is the sacred praxis it begins with. The psalmist says, "He makes me lie down in green pastures; he leads me beside still waters."

I find it beautiful that in the face of terror, God doesn't bid us toward courage as we might perceive it. Instead, he draws us toward fear's essential sister, rest—a sister who is not meant to replace fear but to exist together in tension and harmony with it. For fear's origin is not evil, though evil certainly wields it against our souls daily.

My father says, *Sometimes being afraid can save your damn life.* He pulls my ear into him and mumbles, *Let the fear in, just don't let it run you.* Just as it can be the threatening hand that holds you in bondage, it can also protect you when the journey toward liberation requires perceptive choice and a certain instinct in the face of the unknown. No one would deny it is a good thing that we are terrified to jump from building to building. Fear steadies our impulses and warns us of danger. You might consider it more akin to a watchman than an enemy. And, of course, there is a fear that leans more toward awe than terror. A kind of delight. Your gut plummets within you as you drop from a bungee cord. The drum of a heart turning corners in a corn maze.

I believe fear has the holy potential to draw out awe in us. To lead us into deeper patterns of protection and trust. To mold us into people engaged in the unknown, capable of making mystery of it instead of terror.

. . .

You know about the holes? The ones in my eyes that made me believe I could see air? I came to learn that the mystery of them is grounded in a decay more sinister than we first believed.

The surgeon flops the pictures against the screen and shows me my own eyes lit up in reds and oranges and greens. It looks like beauty to me. Luminous magic tendrils, a landscape of veins and valleys in a glow-in-the-dark leaf. He's looking at me, and I'm thinking, *Behold. Don't you see my glow-veined eyes? Aren't they something to see?* But he exhales a gust that could pierce my heart, and he wrings his own hands out like dirty rags before pointing at the photos. *This is what it* should *look like,* he says, pointing to an eye that doesn't belong to me. *Now this is you.*

He gives me a tour of all the holes ripping through my retinas. He tells me they are too thin for my age. He tells me they're fragile, vulnerable—something about wallpaper and how mine is disintegrating. I nod and wince with him like I understand, as this sunken-faced doctor tells me that my eyes will see many surgeries to preserve my vision as long as we can. By the time these words are published, they will have seen at least four.

Disintegration is no stranger to me. It started with my shoulder and then my arm. My hands. My neck. And then it wandered into my legs from the toes up—sometimes a burning pain, sometimes a numbness. At its strangest, it felt like my muscles themselves had nausea. Turns out, they were atrophying. I have been sick for four years with a litany of neurological disorders that refuse to reveal their origin. My neurologist calls me *Mystery*. Maybe at one point I would've found a strange pride in this. But when your body is leaving you, you'd give anything to be perfectly ordinary. I'm prepared to be emptied of complexity. Make me simple—known and understood and obvious. But that isn't my name.

During the worst parts of those years—when the mere act of swallowing became a risk and my body would erupt in pops and twitches just from rolling over—I would lie awake at night and imagine what this anguish might swell to. When I let my bed swallow me for a whole year, more than anything else, it was fear that tied me to my mattress. What will tomorrow feel like? Will my brain go next? How long before my husband tires of detangling my hair? I had fears and desires that are too painful to name even now.

We still don't exactly know why this is happening to my body. Their best guess is that some autoimmune disease that hasn't been named is making my body destroy itself. I believe that if I receive the worst news of it tomorrow, death itself approaching, I would be better off just for knowing. Uncertainty is fear's playground. I don't know how to wade in it and not drown.

To know incessant fear of loss is, in a way, to know the anguish of loss itself. Each day of waiting for death reeks of death itself. Yet your fear keeps you from grieving and is only ever waiting to grieve. There is a point where the waiting can be such a torment to us that we begin to wish for the loss to just come already, believing that maybe then we can finally begin to grieve and release. It changes what you hope for.

Julian of Norwich was ill and waiting to die, but death didn't come for her when she thought it would. On her almost-deathbed she had a series of visions that she later wrote about. I confess I hate her in part, for she did not shrink from her sickness but saw it as a path to God. I'm jealous of this. But more than hating her, I love her so. I love her for letting me behold a form of belief that I so desperately need. A belief mixed with a relentless truth-telling. I love her for bearing witness to her mortality, for inviting me into her ailing body and all the glory that it wrought. When things get bad in me, I think of her as I lie in bed all day, and I know, for all my love, I am nothing like her. She said:

> If there is anywhere on earth a lover of God who is always kept safe, I know nothing of it, for it was not shown to me. But this was shown: that in falling and rising again we are always kept in that same precious love.

The ancient answer to fear is the recognition that to be human is to be vulnerable—to pain, to suffering, to death itself. In part, fear gets its breath because deep down we believe we were meant for one thing and will receive another. But we should not blame ourselves for hoping. And it doesn't mean we should adopt the simple mantra of *Nothing has been promised to me.*

Whether by God or ancestor or friend, there are promises that reside within each of us. My sister looks me in the eyes and tells me, *You will not go blind. I will not let you go blind.* It's a vow that I rationally know she is incapable of making, yet this promise will still hold me if my vision goes and I come to the end of my seeing before I am ready. My practice is to not let the promise agitate my deepest anxieties. I do not consider deeply whether her vow will be kept; rather my practice is to rest in the love that compelled her to make such a promise.

When Julian speaks not of safety but of love, it reminds us that our fears are often not best met with rationality or even an unveiling of what future's to come. I still see clear bubbles and cobwebs dancing in every light place I look. The most loving thing to be said is *Close your eyes. Go to sleep already.* You will do what you can until you can't, and then you'll fall asleep on the chests of those who love you.

Find those who tell you, *Do not be afraid,* yet stay close enough to tremble with you. This is a love.

. . .

I once worked for a small organization that was sick with fear. People flitted around afraid of disrupting the narrative of organizational goodness. It became a community that operated and dreamed only out of this. It made for very suspicious humans. Secrets began to spill out in elevators and during supervision coffees. It was less a fear of being fired and more a fear of alienation and exclusion. What will happen if I . . . ?

And then the tribes emerged. In fact, tribalism is too noble a word. There were factions—the loyal and the "agitators" (also referred to as "not a good fit"). Any member who challenged the power structure became at risk of being cast out—of opportunities, of leadership, of the inner circle. No threat was overt, but you somehow always knew what was coming if you were not counted as loyal.

In communities of fear, a kind of sectarianism emerges. People group together by allegiances because there is power in numbers. You will find it in communities as small as a household and as vast as a society. A fear that demands a loyalty from you. And fear's economy is so scarce, you must choose whom to be afraid for and whom to hope for. Then you steady yourself on the relentless accumulation of power, never realizing that stealing power doesn't diminish your fear, it only increases it.

In fear communities, the source of the threat can be so woefully oblique that you turn against something or some *other* that you can grab hold of. It convinces you that the path to safety, security, and rest is not love but violence or rejection. The situation becomes gravest when the fear erodes your capacity to hold hope for anyone but your sect.

Tyrants thrive in communities of fear. They deceive the fearful into believing they will resolve their agony. They'll promise safety, power, belonging to those who require their hope be attached to a person, usually a person of status. But as tyrants gain confidence, they have less need to obscure their evil. They learn they can threaten, insult, and abuse their followers directly and openly, past the point of rebuke. They have become salvation to some sect of the community. And in their terror, who would dare rebuke the rescuer?

It's precisely people and communities like this that make me cringe at the phrase "fear the Lord." To me, this hearkens to every abuse-formed relationship with those in power I've witnessed. Those who demand a reverence rooted in fear and not integrity. I don't want to be afraid of God. I don't think this is what is being asked of us. I hope it's not.

Of the many unsung heroines in the Bible, I am drawn to the story of Shiphrah and Puah. They were Hebrew midwives whom Pharaoh ordered to kill every male Hebrew baby at birth. In holy defiance, they delivered every child safely, and when confronted by their tyrant, they looked him in the eye and lied to his face. *Hebrew women are strong,* they told him. *They give birth before we can get to them.* Their rebellion is a model for our liberation today. Perhaps to fear God is to refuse to submit to the demagogues of this world, to refuse to grant them the power they crave, and to place our waiting in the hand of God, who won't manipulate and wield our fears against us but will hold them in tenderness.

. . .

It was a strange act of tenderness when the woman who was not my gramma's mother made her a perfectly beautiful yellow dress and presented it to her on her sixth birthday. It had been a relatively good year financially, and though they couldn't afford to buy new clothes, the woman was a gifted seamstress. It was this sunny yellow fabric with a hand-stitched lace collar hugging the neck and shoulders. She slipped the fancy garment over my gramma's cocoa velvet skin and smiled. *I was beautiful,* my gramma says. *I felt worth something.* And then that woman told her to go show the man who was not her father her dress. *He's in the basement. Go on down to the basement.* As she tells me this now, my gramma smiles at me but not her smile, and my scalp shivers. She said she went running down those stairs that day. And there in her golden dress, my small, hopeful little-girl gramma twirls.

And the man gets real close and tells her today they're going to play a special game.

She looks away from me now and brings her shoulders to her ears and says, *That was the first day he touched me.*

She went upstairs after it was over and had to pretend all day that she hadn't just learned what shame was. They let some folks from church come over, people who thought the man was holy and always said so because he was their deacon. And on Saturday, he took his place at the front, on the right hand of the pastor, and as my gramma sat carved into her wooden pew, she lost her body and tried to not look. When his gaze finally summoned her and they locked eyes—him in his throne and she hollowed out in wood—she said she knew in that moment that God could not protect her.

I now know I was afraid. But back then, it didn't feel like fear. It was dying. Ain't no place to hide when the devil built the house.

My gramma had to live with her tyrants. They cultivated that tiny community of fear behind drawn shades and empty smiles. Tiptoeing down hallways and watching the doorknob. Her home was made of mortar and terror. A prison that hung on her bones even after escaping.

For those of us who know ongoing trauma, we become so used to having fear in our bodies that it is hard to see that it has made its home in us. When you have felt chronically unsafe in your own home, the safest things can feel like terror. My gramma still sleeps with her door open, so if anything happens, someone will hear her crying.

I got demons, she says. But I tell her she doesn't have demons; she's met one.

In time she has reclaimed her body. The fear has not left her altogether, nor if it did would she be stronger for it, but the fear is not ruler to her. In a slow and excruciating miracle, little by little, she excavated this tyrant's evil from her mind. And as true love was lavished on her, the way her child-self should've been loved, the way her seventy-three-year-old self is worthy to be loved, she learns that her fear does not preclude her from hope.

We stave off fear in its most dangerous forms when we allow our agony to be held safely by a number of others. Turning on the light doesn't make the monsters disappear from under our beds, but it reminds us who has power over the switch. Sometimes watching someone else flip the switch liberates your own hands to do likewise.

Who will tremble with you when you feel your insides pressing against your chest and your hands start to dance and your voice becomes another voice? Who will put you to sleep? You are not foolish to fear. You are foolish not to. When you've seen monsters, the holes, the flesh of this world peeled back and bloody . . . we're all shaking.

EIGHT

Lament

On the day she finally left that small, crooked farmhouse on Cemetery Lane, she didn't look back even once. If she did, my gramma, made pillar of salt, would've seen a single spark fly from her breast and saunter over to the roof that so desperately needed to be replaced. And she would've seen the glow start from the top and make its way down to its foundations until the whole place was aflame. If she returned, she would find it to this day still burning. The sound of her own wails rushing to meet her in the clearing.

They knew before she did. Sick at dawn but glowing. The woman who was not her mother told her she was going to be a mother. And the man. The cruel and cowardly man told the church. Everyone knew, but no one said. That the new pulse swelling her womb came from the man who was not her father but was still family and was still supposed to protect her. She was fifteen, and they told her she couldn't sing in the choir anymore or sit with any of the other kids. She was fifteen. She was fifteen.

My blood and a name. That's all I could give to that child. They gave him to a family connected to the church. She made up stories about the boy and this new family—who danced in the kitchen and never hit him with fly swatters when he least expected it. And the man kept coming at night. And the woman kept pretending. And nothing changed and still everything did. And then she left.

An angel from church helped her enroll at a little Seventh-day Adventist school near D.C. *I didn't want to be there,* she says. Then she levitates her eyebrows for a moment and adds, *But I didn't want to be anywhere.*

Her body went to class, but her mind was still in the basement. She spent most of that strange pilgrimage trying to pretend that she was okay. Trying to seem like her cares were the same as everyone else's cares and that she wasn't haunted. But when she sat in church with her hair pressed and her ruffled bobby socks on, and they opened their hymnbooks, all she saw was the man who was not her father staring back at her.

Back then, I used to tear things apart. Whether paper or clothing or even her own lips, she would rip things open absentmindedly. Eventually, her friends began to hand her paper as soon as she walked through the door, and they'd just sit around laughing and chatting as my gramma tore and tore and tore. They did not know what to make of this woman who smiled strange and spoke slowly, like an old woman who was unafraid of running out of time.

One sabbath, after church, she was laughing and joking with her friends and strutting back to the off-campus apartments with everyone all flushed and excitable. But she says she barely made it inside her door before she collapsed on the floor—the charade departing her body, leaving her emptied and sobbing. *I don't know how long I lay there. You can't describe that kind of darkness. Every move, my legs, my arms—it's like it was all weighted down, and you just know, no one is ever gonna know or love you.* The shame of what was done to her, the grief of what was taken from her, and the guilt of leaving—it was and is too much to hold. On two occasions she scarfed down handfuls of sleeping pills like she was starving and waited for death, but God himself stuck three holy fingers down her throat and just made her throw up all night. She wanted to disappear, she says. *But sometimes you just don't.*

My gramma used to wonder if God was laughing at how much she suffered. I want to say to her that if there is a God, he saw what happened to her in that dusty basement and hasn't stopped crying since.

. . .

You can't tell me that it doesn't change everything that the one who created all things and holds together all things cried. If Christ wept for Lazarus, he must've done so not out of an absence of hope or faith, but out of love. It was an honoring. When we weep for the conditions of this world, we become truth-tellers in its defense. People who can say, *This is not good. It is not well.* People who have seen the face of goodness and refuse to call good and curse by the same name.

When Ezra Uche told us that his mother found a lump in her breast one day and was dead two months later, it was Ryan who spoke first and asked if she was "a believer." He held

Ezra's limp hand and said, *Thank God.* He said we *rejoice* because at least she is *home with God. At least she was "saved."*

I am most disillusioned with the Christian faith when in the presence of a Christian who refuses to name the traumas of this world. I am suspicious of anyone who can observe colonization, genocide, and decay in the world and not be stirred to lament in some way. For all the goodness of God, my ancestors were still abducted from their homes, raped, and enslaved. I will not be rushed out of my sorrow for it. And we can delight that God made the garden with all those trees of fruit to feast on, but the earth is ailing and eroding from overconsumption and neglect. I shouldn't need to recite a litany of wounds and injustices and decay in order to justify my sadness. In lament, our task is never to convince someone of the brokenness of this world; it is to convince them of the world's worth in the first place. True lament is not born from that trite sentiment that the world is bad but rather from a deep conviction that it is worthy of goodness.

I can only wonder why we have so many depictions of the cross with Christ looking stoic and resolved and so few with him crying out in pain and abandonment. When I read the story, he does not seem composed; he seems devastated. When we reconstruct a Christ whose very face remains unmoved, how are we to trust that he feels or longs for anything at all? A passionless savior cannot be trusted to save. I have never felt closer to God than when he has tears running down his face. I don't delight in this, but by this, I know that I am seen.

I believe my gramma met God on that linoleum floor in a way many will never encounter him. I don't think this relieved her pain, not really. But I believe she was seen. There is no such thing as a lone wail. Every howl reverberates off the walls of God's chest and finds its way back to us, carrying his own tears with it.

And when God bears witness to our suffering, it is not for his consumption or to demonstrate something. My gramma used to wonder what this all was teaching her, a rhetoric she absorbed from the church. But it seems cruel to believe that God would require grief to make a truth known. I refuse to believe we need to dissect our pain in search of purpose. Sometimes shit is just shit. It's okay to say so.

I think when God bears witness to our lament, we discover that we are not calling out to a teacher but inviting God as a nurturer—a mother who hears her child crying in the night. She wakes, rises, and comes to the place where we lie. She rushes her holy warmth against our flesh and says, *I'm here.*

. . .

There are parts of me I didn't know could tremble. As I walked down that hall, even my fingernails were twitching.

The night before, a call from my little brother had led me down the stairs of our basement, where my parents' room was, to find my father on his bed writhing. I had already called for an ambulance, just like I had already known what my brother would say to me. For my father, my large hero magic father, was also an addict. And on this night, he had taken too much.

As I waited in the hospital to see him, I was cruel and afraid—cruel to my friend who sat quietly chewing his lips off and cruel to my stepmom who did not sit quietly. She told me that I had to beg him to get help. *If you ask, he'll listen.* And I have never known a feeling like walking down that hospital hall, approaching his room. Each step was a death. My stepmom went in first, and before I passed through the doorframe there was a pause that I lived years within. In that time, I took myself back down to that basement—my father cuddling me and bringing me Italian ice to soothe my throat after I had my tonsils taken out. We're watching a *Dateline* special ranking unsanitary fast-food chains, and laughing like it's as good as stand-up. I'm in between his legs and he's laying grease on my scalp.

And then it's the night before and he's writhing again. He's calling out for me.

In that pause in the threshold, I was not afraid my father would refuse to go to rehab. I was not afraid he would never come home again. I was not afraid of seeing him "this way"; I had seen him in the basement dark. I was afraid of him seeing me. Of us seeing each other and knowing once and for all that a profound veil between us had just been torn. Him seeing me see him. An illusion asunder, and I could no longer rouse my belief in it in order to keep him upright. He would have to watch his daughter recognize her father outside the myth of his heroism. Laid bare in a hospitable bed with shaking limbs and missing teeth. This is a sadness that catches you in the throat and doesn't ever really let go. In that pause between me and him, I held on to a former life. My breath began to rattle, my heart into my throat, and I thought just this: People shouldn't live in basements.

My father says we're the same because we both only feel behind closed doors. Like when a cut doesn't hurt until you look down and see the bleeding. After he was hospitalized, I stopped going to class for weeks. I was so avoidant that I didn't even email or withdraw, I just stopped going. In that time, I kept going to church, but I didn't tell a soul for months. I did not trust them to hold my pain in raw form.

Too often I have heard people's pain met with a Christian consolation which essentially communicates that the person in pain should learn to cling to hope, to trust in God. More often than not, I've found this unhelpful, and at worst a form of spiritual abuse that uses language of hope to manipulate the hurting into a feigned happiness.

This is also a foundational misrendering of lament. Lament is not anti-hope. It's not even a stepping-stone to hope. Lament itself *is* a form of hope. It's an innate awareness that what is should not be. As if something is written on our hearts that tells us exactly what we are meant for, and whenever confronted with something contrary to this, we experience a crumbling. And in the rubble, we say, *God, you promised.* We ask, *Why?* And how could we experience such a devastation if we were not on some mysterious plane, hoping for something different. Our hope can be only as deep as our lament is. And our lament as deep as our hope.

Now there is a distinction to be made between true lament and the more sinister form of sadness we know as despair. Despair is lament emptied of hope. It is a shell that invites the whole of your soul to dwell in its void. Many of us will visit this shell, but despair depends upon our staying. With no framework for healthy lament, I was a prisoner to sadness.

Even still, it's not good to drag someone from their lament out of fear of despair. In fact, being forced too quickly out of lament can drag the soul into despair in secret. We are left to wander in sadness but without a confidant to help guide us out of the void.

We will not heal divorced from our emotions. A spirituality that depends on positivity will lead not only to emotional fallacies but also eventually to delusions of all kinds. Hundreds of thousands of people can march for miles declaring Black Lives Matter, and you will find it so disruptive to your delusion of positivity that you will not become curious or sensitive. Instead, you will find yourself defensive of the fallacy. You can listen to the story of someone's depression, and your instinct will be to find silver linings so that you yourself feel some kind of resolve. People whose faiths are predicated on happiness make for dangerous friends and woefully disconnected fellow humans.

Sometimes denial of pain is born of self-preservation. In bearing witness to sadness, you may find yourself confronted with questions like *Who is responsible? Am I to blame? What are you saying about my grandfather?* Our histories, stories, and sins render us so defensive of our delusions of good selves that we are unable to see the tears of another clearly. This can function on the communal level, too, as entire countries convince themselves of a positive hero image, drowning out the cries of those around the world with anthems and stories of the nation's greatness. The church is not exempt from this.

At some point, you must ask yourself, are you so committed to the delusion of positivity that you will stand by unmoved as those who bear the image of God cry out in pain? Will you walk past the tears of Christ, pretending not to notice? Or worse, will you tell him to get up from the linoleum floor and *hope* in God?

Sometimes I think that if some Christians stopped talking about escaping a someday hell and started bearing witness to the hellish conditions of life and the world at present, they'd see a lot more people in their churches come Sunday. When I watch somebody name what should not be and earnestly question God about it, I immediately become a fraction of the skeptic I am. Lament is a very compelling apologetic.

I don't know if I've encountered better emotional truth-telling than when visiting Black churches. Black people of faith know how to wail. And they know how to crack up. I once watched a preacher start dancing as he prayed. His voice was shaky and syncopated. A runaway child had returned, and everyone was howling and celebrating. But as the prayer went on, he ran out of breath and just started crying and softly beating his fist to chest. When the music stopped, his fist was still beating, and everyone mirrored him as the room quieted. It felt pure to me. If there was any performance in it, it was the kind of art that is for healing and not for consumption. When it's not being consumed, Black lament is something to behold. Some churches know how to shake the numbness from your flesh.

. . .

He said they used to steal cars like they were taking the bus. On the weekends, my dad and Corey would jump one and drive it a minute up the way from the roller rink and walk the rest. If they needed a ride home, they'd just jump another and head back.

One night, Mario gets a Trans Am and picks my dad and Corey up to go party in Homewood. They go to get ready first, find a little buzz before leaving. But then two bright Black angels show up, who my father and Corey would rather get drunk with, so they decide to stay behind. Mario dips without them and goes to pick up a few others, and they're speeding down East Carson. *I mean fast, too damn fast,* my father tells me, hugging himself. And before Mario's body can hear his mind screaming, he collides with another car, an elderly couple, and as soon as their noses touch, the cars become one and explode. Everyone died in the fire except Roger, who caught an air underneath him as he went soaring out of the crumpled metal and landed off away and alone. Roger ended up in a coma and then in the hospital for years after that night. *We were just with him,* my father says. *I should be dead.*

It wasn't until Tuesday, when my father watched the *Challenger* space shuttle explode seventy seconds after takeoff, that he finally felt an agony stir in him. In that moment, when the whole world inhaled sharply and fell silent, my father bowed his head and screamed. There, sitting alone on the edge of his bed, while the world grieved seven mighty space heroes, my father wept for his own. For Mario, and for the night chariot that in the end belonged to him. You might think the sadness of the world eclipsed my father's cries, but in mystery, it amplified them.

I don't know what that did to me. It was like someone poured heat all over me and I was burning too. My father didn't know how to grieve for his friend until the whole world stopped and grieved. It is not always instinctual.

A Black woman I admire once drew me into a line from Jeremiah 9:20 that says, "Hear, O women . . . teach to your daughters a dirge, and each to her neighbor a lament." When she told me this, two things occurred to me. The first: Lament is intergenerational. The second: It is something that can be taught.

When I moved to Philly after college, my first friends were a group of nuns. I was leading small groups at a quaint Catholic university, and Sister June, worried that I was lonely but never saying so, would invite me for meals and rosary walks. I went with her a handful of times to a prayer labyrinth that she walked weekly. The first time I went, I thought it would be a maze. I was hoping it would be. But prayer labyrinths aren't meant to trap you, and the goal isn't to get out; it's a journey to the center and back again, and the way is long but clear. It's an ancient practice of embodied meditation. Sister June would mumble to herself as we walked the path from different ends. I'd pick leaves and rip them up into smaller and smaller pieces as I made my way. Sometimes, when Sister June approached the center, she'd begin to cry. I'd linger awkwardly in places to avoid the center while her mumbles became a gentle wailing.

But one time, she just peeked over her shoulder at me and said, *Well, come on, then.* I entered the center with her, and she slid a photo from her skirt pocket and pressed it flat between her two palms without showing me. *My sister,* she said, and she wasn't wiping her tears away. I asked, *Older or younger?* And maybe she knew I just didn't know what else to say, because instead of answering, she said, *I come here to cry for her.* And then, *Let me tell you about her.* We walked the path out together as she told me about their love and the loss and how she once and still sometimes hated God. She told me that as she walks to the center she travels into sadness. As she walks out, she reminds herself that she isn't imprisoned by it.

We are born knowing how to cry, but it takes another to teach us how to cry well and with purpose. As we watch our elders cry, we are learning. Sister June taught me how to grieve with my body. She taught me how to feel the tears on my face and not wipe them away. Her rhythm of lament has settled into my soul. At Wisewood, we're collecting stones now to make a prayer labyrinth in the field next to the house.

I walk the path and whisper to myself, *You are no shell*. I make the pilgrimage into my deepest sorrows, knowing tragedy doesn't own me. *Your wails are worthy to be heard*. Journey to the center with me now; together, we won't get lost in despair. Your wails are worthy to be heard.

Aren't your eyelids
Tired of keeping
Prisoners? Those tears
Are precious
Minerals. Lap them up
Like a medicine—
It's called healing.

NINE

Rage

The teacher slapped a face on the projector, and all the white girls snapped their gum and winced, and the white boys knocked elbows with wide eyes and murmurs, and we three—we three Black-bodied souls—we sat there, frozen solid in a gust of something we didn't yet have the language for. As we traced the rips and pits in Emmett Till's face, as we watched him lit up from behind and made bright and large and spectacle, we felt something hot pulse in the space between us.

Our school was Black and white. There were three of us in honors history. But in gym class, there were more of us than them, and that afternoon, I went to the Black-girl side of the locker room. Usually I would linger somewhere on the line between the two, trying not to be noticed as I alternated between the different worlds quietly. On this day, I chose sides. I didn't speak, but I was welcomed. Jazz, who smelled like tea tree oil and quaked when she laughed, braided my hair while I fidgeted and everyone spoke chaotically over and around me. The braids were tight, but I was grateful no one was asking anything of me.

Until one from the other side yelled over, asking if I wanted to be her weights partner. I did not, and I said so. And the Brunette Beast, having noticed a shift in me but lacking the patience or love to wait for me to name it, flung her hair over her shoulder and whispered loudly to her thin-lipped herd, *Whatever, she's mad at us.*

In that moment, I became three things. The first, a seer. It felt as if I could look at someone and the truth of them would rise and pool at their surface. I saw that this girl did not truly believe I was "mad" at them; me not choosing her roused a self-hatred that was dormant in her. The second, an actor. In an instant, I learned to unzip myself, wriggle out of my own skin and into something stiff and smiling. Before allowing myself to be seen by whiteness, I learned to ask, Is it safe here? Can I breathe? *You're good,* I mumbled up to her. *You're good.* And the third, angry. Truly and profoundly angry. Like a fire nestled in my mouth, and when I opened it, the air I was breathing would only feed the flames. Even now, every once in a while, a spark will lick the hem of some long-legged white woman, and when she turns to growl at me, I see the face of the Brunette Beast, and I feel nothing at all.

In the classroom that morning, with the only light emanating from the face of a battered child, I learned what white anger does. What rage must it take to pulverize a child? In demonic fury, to try to crush the image of God in a person? If you can look at what they did to him and feel nothing, you are not numb, you are dead.

And what inner death does it take to allow your own guilt to torment someone else's grief? Far too many people are incapable of bearing witness to someone else's emotions without centering their own. Interestingly enough, I never heard the brunette beast question the anger that would stir those white devils to destroy the face of a child. It was not their anger that disrupted her consciousness, but mine. We should think about this.

There's a story of Jesus coming across a bare fig tree and cursing it, and his disciples just stand there watching it wither away. I wonder what they thought of him—bent on destroying a tree just because it wasn't bearing fruit. This anger once seemed strange and unnecessary to me. I don't think the story makes much sense alienated from its sequel, when Christ goes tearing through the temple, flipping tables. He confronts those meant to be bearers of belonging in the world and calls out the culture of exclusivity and exploitation they're perpetuating instead. It all made sense when I learned that fig tree was the private preface to the very public force of anger in the temple. A place to encounter the divine had become a place of scarcity, emptied of the most vulnerable. And in the face of injustice and exclusion, we meet a God of holy, premeditated, bodily, unapologetic rage.

When people do muster up the courage to talk about this wild demonstration of rage from God, they tend not to name it as such. It is easy to make it more about what was happening in the temple, instead of what was happening in the body of the Christ. What does it mean that Christ doesn't just scream but also physically overturns tables? What does it mean that Christ doesn't just lament the bare fig tree but damns it, leaving his followers with gaping mouths and no immediate resolution?

It should be no secret that Black anger has been demonized by a white-dominated society—white Christianity playing no small part in the subjugation. We are told that the pinnacle of piety is *niceness,* and we are shamed out of conflict, protest, advocacy. We can cry but not too loud, our agony never allowed to disrupt the illusion of unity. I like that God doesn't play or talk nice to the hands of injustice. What freedom it is to witness a God whose primary concern is not for how he makes the oppressor *feel,* but for feeling alongside the oppressed, and telling the truth about it. For so long, Black people, noosed and muzzled, have not been permitted the liberty to tell the truth about the evil we've endured. And now, the language of niceness—and more recently, *civility*—serves to muzzle us further.

There is an evil absurdity in this. I can name very few instances (none, arguably) of a *niceness* in God, and yet this is the demand the oppressor will always make of us. Make no mistake, this is not for our spiritual growth or formation; it is to protect the fragility of the oppressor, who knows that as we unleash the truth of our anger, their conscience and persona will be implicated. Not everyone is prepared for these truths. Audre Lorde said, "I cannot hide my anger to spare you guilt, nor hurt feelings. . . . Guilt is not a response to anger; it is a response to one's own actions or lack of action. If it leads to change then it can be useful, since it is then no longer guilt but the beginning of knowledge." The anger of Black people is the undeserved gift of knowledge. I have no interest in protecting the ignorance of the violent. The most appropriate response to my rage should perhaps be gratitude.

Still, the embrace of my own anger remains complicated.

No matter how many emotions I allow someone to bear witness to, I know I will be reduced to anger. For the majority of my life, this has led me to suffocate myself. I learned how to seem calm. Composure became my most treasured mask. I learned to coddle the egos of those who do great harm. I learned, as Dickinson says, how to "tell all the truth but tell it slant." And most gravely, I learned to never, ever flip the table.

I cast my anger so far out of my own body that for a long time, it forgot how to stomp or scream or throw. On the occasion that I muster enough courage to participate in conflict, I empty it of all emotion. I talk plain and monotone, becoming more machine than human. In time, I have realized my expression of anger is so limited, so chained, that it has actually become less true.

James Baldwin said, "People who shut their eyes to reality simply invite their own destruction, and anyone who insists on remaining in a state of innocence long after that innocence is dead turns himself into a monster." I'm not convinced we can tell the truth alienated from the truth of our emotion. They are necessary company. Sometimes, however threatening it may be, it is seeing the face of anger that can finally shake a people out of their numbness, out of their inner death.

I've determined I will no longer settle for mere articulation of anger. I want to feel my voice shake and the warmth creep up my spine.

. . .

She says, *Mine was a vitriolic anger.*

Growing up on Cemetery Lane, my gramma inhaled bible stories as an escape. *Chile, I grew up on Spam and Daniel and the lion's den*. Her favorite thing to draw was Shadrach, Meshach, and Abednego in the fiery furnace. Until one day it occurred to her: If God can do all that, why couldn't he protect her knees from going raw when she was forced by the woman to kneel on rice and recite the scriptures from memory for hours? Why didn't he double the soup and bread at dinner so she could double Dutch without feeling faint? And why couldn't he protect her from the man who was not her father? *And if he don't care, why don't he just let me die already?* Her belief in the existence of God was durable, which did not reduce her anger but enlarged it.

She left that Seventh-day Adventist school and the church, and tried to leave God himself, but found herself tethered to him by rage. A mercy she did not readily comprehend. But in the end, it is much easier to locate love in rage than in apathy. Apathy is a giving up, a surrendering to what is. And it's inherently a disconnecting force. It moves you away from a person. Rage comes for you. It is inherently relational. It might come with fire, but it's still moving toward something, and in proximity, there is hope for reconnection. In this way, anger itself is a function of reconciliation. It is a bringing together. And it was anger's sacred bond that kept my gramma near to her God.

When we speak of anger, it is important to recognize its praxis as manifold, each expression capable of sacredness in its own right. This may be overly simplistic, but I tend to classify anger practices as interior or exterior. Interior anger is expressed plainly and held unconditionally between you and God. This is cursing the hands that hang the noose. It's dreaming about revenge against those who once hurt you. Exterior anger is made public for others to bear witness to and even be moved by. A crowd of ten thousand marches to the cry of *I can't breathe. Hands up, don't shoot. I can't breathe.*

I remember when I first read the psalmist begging God to break the teeth of his enemies in their mouths. I couldn't believe all the priests and pastors in my life got away with never mentioning this. Anger expressed in the interior life is permitted to exist in its rawest and most honest form. It is not kept private out of shame or because it is inferior in status to public anger. Rather, its privacy grants us the freedom to understand our rage without pressure or compulsion to dilute it. It gives us the space to be laid bare and have our anger, like any emotion, refined in the presence of the divine.

If you read the psalms, you'll find no small number of them committed to rage. Calling for a creditor to seize money from the oppressors, begging for bones to be broken, enemies to be wiped out, their descendants punished. These imprecatory psalms were a liberation to me because they finally told me the truth—that is, I belong to a God capable of holding the ugliest parts of my anger. I never prayed the same again. To be permitted an anger that is imperfect, that tells the truth about the revenge and terror I crave for those who do harm, allows me to see things in myself that might otherwise go unnoticed. So often our wounds are invisible to or neglected by the world, and our anger must be hidden in order to belong or survive. It is very important that our belonging before God not depend upon our ability to hide or extinguish truths in and about us. We must trust that our maker can look on our rage, and even our hatred, and perceive those stories, fears, and vulnerabilities that reside in us and have stirred us toward our present emotional expression. As we allow God to behold our rage, a sacred intimacy emerges.

As we think about the virtue of exterior anger, we should understand it as no more or less holy than interior anger. It is also not a trajectory. Our raw and private anger is not necessarily reborn into public anger. Interior expression of anger is a worthy practice in its own right.

Exterior anger is often in defense of some sphere, person, or piece of creation. Demanding Amazon be held accountable for its environmental impact; interrupting the man who interrupted the woman midthought in a meeting. Anger is never holier than when it acts in defense of the dignity of a person or piece of creation. But it requires we be more measured and protective of our words—not so that we censor ourselves on behalf of the fragile and defensive, but so that we will be heard by those we wish to be heard by. You can be a person of profound anger without allowing it to eclipse your or anyone else's personhood.

But there are times when anger devolves into something more desperate—a hatred that delights in death. My gramma said, *Anger is one thing, but justifiable anger . . . you gotta be careful with this. Because you got every right to hate them.* When anger is justified, it can feel as though when your anger swells, so does justice. This is a danger, for it's very difficult to distinguish rage from hatred. And hatred, which can still be a holy thing if directed toward evils and not creation, is also very fragile. It is difficult to contain it to where it's meant to be.

After she dropped out of college, my gramma started doing

stand-up at private parties. She says she had a knack for just looking at a person and being able to rip them apart. If she saw someone with an ugly dress or who laughed strangely, she would just latch on to them and not let go until they were hurting. She'd end up ditching half of what she planned to say, and everyone else would be howling, but maybe they were just relieved it wasn't them. *I was not a nice, happy person.* For those watching from the sidelines, this was an infectious humor in her. For the targets of her vitriol, it was like having the wind knocked out of you with such a force you couldn't even remember who hit you or what you did to deserve it. For a season, my gramma's anger, justified and sacred, devolved into mere hatred. And it bled into more than she had the energy to protect.

The answer to moments of deformed anger is not to release the practice altogether, but to unalienate it and reintegrate it into an emotionally diverse life. In this season, my gramma could not integrate anger and joy in her person. And when you have room for only one emotion, it begins to masquerade as all the others. Anger wears happiness, and a woman stands in front of her crowd bringing laughter out of hatred.

The more we listen to our own anger, the better a listener it becomes. It becomes less of a weapon and more of a path to greater attunement with our own needs and desires. If we do not starve our anger of attention, of affection, of intimacy, we will seldom find it desperately clamoring to take up space where it wasn't meant to. An anger that is confident in its own belonging doesn't need to compete to be held. Its hope becomes not for its own survival, but for the life of the soul that bears it.

. . .

It should not come as a surprise that nations built on Black suffering do not now recognize Black emotion with any particularity. Black anger has been forced into hiding by whip and chain and hose for so long that when whiteness encounters Black emotionality now, it still feels thoroughly alien. Whiteness can only wonder why we grimace when it has demanded a skull bowed and smiling. And for a people who have rarely practiced or processed their own rage well, it can only be deeply threatening to see anger operating elsewhere, even if that anger is ever so righteous and necessary for the life and dignity of the world. Whiteness's rage cannot conceive of such an anger, because it has never known it in itself.

Bus stops can be crucibles for suffering. I'm splitting a metal-netted bench with a Black mom with her hair in flat twists and shadows resting under her eyes. She has five or six plastic bags slung from her arms, and every time she lifts them to point and tell her son to *get back over here* or *quit that,* the handles dig into her flesh, leaving glistening dents behind from the pressure and sweat. We spot the bus coming up the hill just as one of the bags cracks itself open on the concrete. We haven't said a word to each other, but now we're rushing around together grabbing cans and markers gone rolling. Two chip bags catch wind and float away like a tragedy, and we're doing our best.

She grabs her son by the hood as we scurry on the bus like pirates, and we start squeezing and moving toward the open seats in the back. And the boy must've brushed up against him, because this guy cuts his palm through the air and tells him to watch it. The woman is still clutching two cans of beans and a box of Goldfish when she says he better watch his mouth. And I don't know how it got here, but his auburn beard is inching closer and closer to her tired face, and he's pushing his bag into the kid like he doesn't see him, and I reach out from behind and squeeze my hand in between the corner of the man's bag and the kid's chest, separating the two. And the woman is saying, *Man, get out of here with all that, man.* But he keeps going as the passengers bow their heads. The woman cocks her head to one side and opens her eyes wider, and she's saying, *I am not the one,* which is Black for "don't start right now." *I am not the one,* and I know she sure as hell isn't, but she can't show him so because her son is there and she can't afford not to center his protection now.

Another man finally gets beard-man to sit down, but he's still muttering like a coward, and we're pretending not to notice, collecting her strewn goods in a seat between us. And we feign a little laughter here or there, but the whole time she's squeezing the kid in between her legs with a force, and he doesn't fight it. But their stop comes, and just as they're shuffling toward the doors, ignoring the man who now seems to be ignoring them, he sends some spit flying right toward the ground where the mom is walking. I see a few stray sprinkles land on the little boy's hood. I stand up, and I turn to fire. I'm yelling and my voice is shaking, and my hands become my fathers', arcing and diving through the air like a dance. And he's looking embarrassed and I'm feeling tall. I'm a tower. My voice is shaking, but I'm standing.

I remember how my body felt on that bus, but I couldn't tell you what I said. All I know is by the next stop, my throat was raw, my hands were trembling from the inside, and I wasn't on the bus anymore.

White anger is something else. It can spit on a kid and still appear victim enough to have someone else thrown off the bus. White rage, like all rage born not in defense of dignity but in defense of oppressive power, is manipulative. It is one of many examples of the difference between anger that dominates and anger that liberates. Admittedly, I remain unsure of how much of each my bus-rage contained.

Anger that dominates relies on fear tactics and abuse to live. It makes no demand of the world except that it bow. This is often because it fears being ruled or overpowered itself. This is no excuse. Holy anger is that which liberates. It marches, chants, and flips tables, demanding wrong be called by its rightful name. It is both passion and calculation, longing for more but for the sake of justice and dignity.

It is easy to mistake oppressive anger for holy anger when you believe that you are worthy of more than someone else, that your dignity depends on this. And even easier in a society that holds up an inflated sense of self for some and diminishes it in others. A mob of eight hundred insurrectionists storm the U.S. Capitol, and they are handled with great sympathy. But a Black man takes a knee during the national anthem, and it's equated to treason.

I don't remember what I said to the man on the bus. But I'm glad fifteen to twenty people bore witness to it. I hope they remember my face and the way my voice shook and with what speed I stood. Some buses are harder to stand up in. But in order to be free, truly free, you have to fight. Our liberation depends on our ability to unlearn the lies told about our own anger. Those who tell the lie are afraid of a world where the oppressed are grounded in their anger—where they recognize their subjugation and believe fully, in their bodies, in private and in public, this is not okay.

So I pray you scream. May a harsh blood beat through every limb, with a sound loud enough to shatter glass. Poke the beast. Burn it down. Do not smile for them. They who destroy and use anger to dominate, they deserve nothing from you. Look them in their scared, miserable eyes, and tell the truth with the passion it demands. Tell them, *I am not the one.*

TEN

Justice

My father says it started off with them rapping against each other. *Just performing. Talent shows and break dancing and shit*. He says I would've laughed at it—the neighborhood crews facing off against each other *like we were about something*.

They would meet in the street, taking turns stepping into the circle to twist and juke and clown. The other crew would try their best to look unimpressed, nudging and mumbling to one another but, every once in a while, erupting in excitement when someone hit a move just right. It started as play. And they were really just kids who needed something to be a part of.

I ask him what changed.

He says, *Then crack came.*

This is what he says: *A lot of people don't know what crack did. Maybe you're broke, but you can always buy a five-dollar rock, one of those little pieces of soap—once you tried it, you didn't stop. And you weren't better than the next person. You could go out and make more money in an afternoon than your parents made in a month. Think about that,* he says.

I hadn't.

No really, think about that. If you see your mom working eight hours during the day and another job at night, and still coming home and saying we gotta have peanut butter sandwiches for dinner, but you, a kid, know you can go out and bring home steaks. What are you going to do? Really think about that. What are you going to do?

I pause for a moment, then say, *I'm selling.* And he winces and smiles, dipping his head like he's paying his respects.

He says the streets went from dancing to fighting to selling. It went from stealing purses to shooting up houses. *And if a circle formed, your ass did not want to be in the center of it anymore.* He had a choice to make, and no man can rightfully be the judge of it. With my gramma busy trying to hold up the sky, my father had no supervision. He made his choice when no one was looking.

It was the Fourth of July, and he and Corey were in Corey's living room in a cirrus cloud of weed. And his dad's girlfriend came rushing in with her glasses half off her face, begging for help with the bathroom door. They bolted for the bathroom, and my father, forgetting where he began and Corey ended, started wordlessly flinging theirself against the door with the force of a rip current tearing away from shore. When they finally broke down the door, they found Corey's father frozen midmelt between tub and toilet. He had overdosed.

And you are no better.

We cannot trust a society that makes judgments on the morality of a person without taking responsibility for how its own morality has instigated the conditions that call for such desperate decision-making. There are those who would say that Corey's father, and my father, and the crew they ran the streets with, deserved punishment. This is a society that will very rarely demand justice in favor of the desperate but will always demand it in favor of the judge, the powerful. In the company of these tainted moral authorities, the most significant wrong will never be the one that caused all the others.

This is a world that demonizes those who transgress the system but has great sympathy for the system itself. You can ask my father why he, who cradled the head of his best friend's father on the bathroom floor that day, lived to hustle. But will you also question the system, which demanded his hustle in order to live? His justice has been denied since birth, so before you fault him, you must first fault this.

There comes a point when we must ask ourselves who the judge is and how they came to be in that position. And then still, who never gets passed the gavel? From bell hooks: "Justice is different from violence and retribution; it requires complex accounting." When Tupac said only God could judge him, this was not mere bombast; it was naming the truth that no one else can be trusted to judge, to do this "accounting," certainly not the ones whose greed and systemic oppression is the impetus for our desperate rule breaking. It is not that society needs good judges so much as that *we* must become *honest* judges, capable of understanding our own hand in the injustices that we have been charged to address.

You cannot tell the story of injustice without telling the story of power. It requires integrity to become honest about how our power systems and our position in the world affect our capacity to do justice. Which is to say, justice can never be severed from mercy. The two sway and balance each other as we move into the stories of our and others' wrongs.

And that power which is stolen, malformed, or inequitable will, no matter how well intentioned, always cast its weight in the wrong places. This is rarely accidental. Injustice has survived by cowering behind the guises of morality and ethics. The whole charade is diabolical. True justice has little concern for good and bad, and is much more interested in protecting and affirming dignity with tangible actions and repair.

You might think justice is a form of choosing sides, choosing whom to stand behind. In a way, maybe it is. But justice doesn't choose whose dignity is superior. It upholds the dignity of all those involved, no matter whom it offends or what it costs. Even when demanding retribution, justice does not demean the offender's dignity; it affirms it. It communicates that what has been done is not what the offender was made for. They, too, were made for beauty. In justice, everyone becomes more human, everyone bears the image of the divine. Justice does not ask us to choose.

For me, there is no liberation without justice. They are not the same, but they depend on one another. An enslaved person, while they are enslaved, will never know justice. Just because the master lets you live in the house doesn't make you any freer. In these cases, it is not justice that is being granted but aid—often born of the guilt of the captor. Make no mistake, if you are not free, it is not justice. I do not celebrate crumbs when I know of the bread that has been promised to me.

I think about how God didn't just rescue Moses and his

people from Pharaoh; he sent plagues until Pharaoh agreed, and when Pharaoh reneged, he drowned an army in the sea. The freedom of God's people did not occur in a vacuum. There were consequences. There was truth-telling. And there was a disturbingly costly justice. There could be no liberation without it.

You might ask yourself if you can ever really be free if you have not received justice for your bondage. But as Bayard Rustin said, "When an individual is protesting society's refusal to acknowledge his dignity as a human being, his very act of protest confers dignity on him."

Justice does not always come in the manner we long for, but there is always a path to it.

. . .

When a quarter million souls swelled the National Mall to hold the dream of Martin Luther King, Jr., my gramma was eighteen and she was there. She piled onto the weathered church bus and spilled out into the lungs of the crowd—groans and gasps flitting through the air between every body. Martin's deep gust of a voice hemming them all in like a force field. And as she stood there in the presence of great Blackness—one cell in the landscape of veins and arteries pumping the same Black blood—she did not become smaller but larger.

She heard a crack in her knee joints, and her bones began to stretch out under her until the Washington Monument looked like a mere nail broken free from its blue coffin. For a moment the crowd around her faded, and she made her way to the edge of the Reflecting Pool. She exhaled and let herself fall backward, the water overtaking her new largeness. When she emerged she was not alone. A baptism born of belonging. She says, *I didn't realize there were that many Black people in the world*. For her it was a first awe. *The first time I really realized that there were enough of us. That we were a movement. That we deserved more.*

Soon, she began going to protests: for Blackness, for an end to the Vietnam War, for an end to Blackness in the Vietnam War. She was not a leader so much as she was a keeper. She'd go around marches and protests to document the young people pouring in, taking down their names along with their parents' names and phone numbers, so that if, God forbid, anything went down, someone in the crowd would know who some of them belonged to.

The fight was new to her. On the day Dr. King was murdered and the riots started, she called the woman who was not her mother to let her know she was okay, and the woman had no idea what my gramma was even talking about. That small town in Pennsylvania was an island. There they were raised to be *one of the good ones*—unfastened from the movement. She says white folk were pleased with them in the way one appreciates a dog who no longer pisses in the house. In this way, and many other ways, leaving was her salvation. A rebirth into belonging to her Blackness without apology.

Activism is the body of justice. It invites you into embodied declarations of dignity and worth. As you participate in its body, you find yourself increasingly grounded in your own.

I think activism is a virtue. To be a person who cares and honors creation is to be a person who acts in favor of its flourishing. I am distrustful of spiritual people who are not roused in their bodies on behalf of justice. We can disagree on what activism should look like, but not on the necessity of its existence or your participation in it.

Those who resist activism tend to do so out of self-preservation, fear, or comfort. For me, it was the fear. Something of my selfhood, which has always been given to stillness and the mind, was terrified of being unable to locate my belonging in intellectualism. I believed that to be calm and disembodied was a kind of enlightenment. Or, more truthfully, I dismissed the deeper belief, which is: I'm not brave enough to fight. And so I inflated projects of the mind as superior in order to shield myself from what I felt was a profound inferiority.

A mentor and friend once said to me, *If there is someone who is both activist and contemplative and who does both well, I have not yet met them.* I silently accepted the challenge. He was articulating a very credible tension between the heart of the contemplative and the heart of the activist. At first strike, they appear inherently in conflict. The contemplative, some pillar of stillness, tasked with thinking and asking enduring questions that require a kind of slowness and pause. The activist, a beacon for the movement, committed to the doing of justice and mercy—not later but now, which does, as the name suggests, require action.

But what if what we take as stillness is not always inactivity as we perceive it? Can there be a form of contemplation that is at once stillness and movement? Some might say the beginnings of Christian monasticism were, in part, a defiant protest against the elitism and centering of the upper class in the faith. And today, activism tells the truth about what is and imagines what should be. This imagination for justice requires contemplation.

For quite some time, the only portraits of activism I had were Dr. King and Malcom X. Marches, rallies, sit-ins—holy embodiments that should be respected deeply, for they protect and guide us today. But the first time I picked up James Baldwin, I finally saw myself. It occurred to me that I could be an activist from my own source of power—words.

It can only make our journey toward justice more robust, more beautiful, when we offer a diversity of paths, a more expansive vision of action. This is not new. This is Detour and Hiero Veiga's graffiti art resurrecting Black faces slain by the police. This is Tricia Hersey and The Nap Ministry creating collective sleeping experiences to reclaim the justice and liberation in rest. This is even, to some degree, some of the words you'll find in this book. Written in holy defiance of what is, and in imagination of what should be. If writing is a calling, I have a responsibility to demand justice in my writing as much as in the streets. When we expand our imaginations for activism, we enter into practices of lament and rage with more particularity, and we begin to realize more nuanced paths to justice.

I once interviewed an international political cartoonist named Pedro X. Molina for *Sampsonia Way,* a literary magazine that amplifies the voices of persecuted writers and artists. Pedro and his family had recently fled Nicaragua to escape the violence of the Ortega-Murillo regime. He taught me about using humor as resistance, sharing stories of how the people of Nicaragua began to protest the regime in their own ways. In

December of 2018, hundreds of people had been killed by the paramilitaries in the streets, and the people were becoming increasingly afraid of going out to protest. So, at one point, large groups of people took a ton of white and blue balloons (the colors of the national flag), inflated them, and released them on the streets in the middle of the night. The next morning, they stood at their windows, laughing, watching these suited-up guys in military clothing and with AK-47s slipping and struggling to step on all of the balloons. Pedro said, *What can I offer as a human being to this world? I can offer my discontent. I can offer my humor. I can offer my particular way of expressing myself through art.*

Pedro also said, *But every time . . . the violence grows, it gets harder and harder to find something to laugh at.*

Activism that commits to bearing witness to injustice can be weary work. It should come as no surprise, for we were never meant to need to look upon and travel so deeply into inequity. Seeing a person or piece of creation trampled should always disrupt something in us. It should always do something to the soul. And when you trace that trampling back across generations and systems and powers, a quiet sorrow is born in you.

I've always appreciated the audacity of the prophet Habakkuk, who, in weariness and frustration, demanded God do something about the corrupt leadership of the time and the people's extortion and oppression at the hands of the wealthy. He told God to say something. This is an honorable demand. To me, it is not an oversimplification to say the Christian story is the tension between the promise of justice and liberation and the unjust and oppressive patterns in our daily lived experiences. I simply cannot comprehend the gospel outside of this.

Perhaps you've heard it said that justice delayed is justice denied. Maybe that's why Christ died in the middle of time and not as a culmination. Maybe God knew if restoration was delayed any longer, the hope of it would be lost altogether.

But as creation lingers on, we still require countless other acts of liberation as we do justice alongside the God who began it. As we fail, we become less and less human, until eventually we cannot be trusted to even distinguish virtue from vice, oppressor from oppressed. As Assata Shakur said, "Nobody in the world, nobody in history, has ever gotten their freedom by appealing to the moral sense of the people who were oppressing them." Societies dominated by an oppressor cannot trust those in power to discern justice from injustice. It has taken them too long. They are parched and delirious, their memory of themselves tainted. Their only hope is to hear the voices of the marginalized guiding them back to water—a mercy that they will not immediately understand. It is not until they drink from the streams that the prophet Amos calls on to roll down like justice and righteousness that their withering souls regenerate, and they recognize that all this time, the problem was not that they were thirsty; it was that they were cursed.

Alice Walker says, "Only justice can stop a curse." I once recited this to a person who took great and immediate offense. *What about love? I'd replace justice with love.* I thought it tragically bizarre that she could perceive love without justice, or justice without love. To me, it's the same word in a different language. Justice without love is oppression. There will always be one party who doesn't immediately perceive the deepest acts of justice as a love. But this is not our responsibility.

. . .

I saw the face of God in a sugarcane field.

We had gone to the Dominican Republic in the name of relief and salvation. It was an arrogance that led us there. We rode in cattle trucks through seas of leafy green until the *batey,* the village, materialized like a tin glacier bobbing with its roots tilting beneath it.

Mottled throughout the head-high emerald cane were patches of ash black, where workers burned the stalks before harvest. Swinging above the scorched earth were dozens of machetes too rusted to reflect the sky. But if you looked closer still, you could make out the dozens of Black bodies holding them, hidden in the acres stretching out to the horizon. They arced their blades with both gracefulness and force, the sound of the slicing creating its own rhythm. Their movement was beautiful to me, and I watched them like they were onstage.

Only they didn't want to be there.

Those tiny sacred sugarcane villages were made of Haitian migrant workers. Undocumented, they were at the mercy or lack of mercy of whatever Dominican bound them to the cane in a despairing form of modern slavery. That Dominican usually bound by powerful white men who sit comfortably at the helm of some billion-dollar sugar company—and those men bound by their own hunger. Manolo, our translator, told me that some of those men and boys would spend the whole of their lives trying to work off a debt that never really ends.

On our third day there, I was wrist-deep in suds and the tightly wound curls of a little girl named Magalie. A group of us who weren't qualified to help in the pop-up medical or dental clinics had set up a makeshift salon, washing and braiding hair. I was massaging the tiny scabs on Magalie's scalp and listening to the older women hum when a woman brought her daughter over to me. She tapped the girl's mouth and it flung wide open. She pointed inside.

I saw it immediately but didn't understand what I was seeing.

Coiling through the shadow of her mouth, a brown, bark-like root was bursting from the crown of a molar, like she had popped a twig in her mouth one day and forgot to chew. I traced the sharpness of my own molar. I closed her mouth. It bounced open again like an eye blinking, and I wanted one of us to disappear, though I wasn't sure who.

I fumbled out in poor Spanish that I wasn't one of the dentists. I must've said it wrong because she just kept pointing to the twig, so I grabbed the mother's hand, and she placed the little girl's hand in my other hand, and for the smallest moment as we transitioned, we formed a circle that was at once awkward and necessary. I walked them to the edge of the dental tent, motioning with my chin, afraid to let go first. They released me abruptly, and I turned and walked straight into the cane, lurking as the howls from the tent followed me into the green.

When I got back to the compound that afternoon, I cried in the shower and then wandered around glaring at all the other Americans as if *they* had planted the seed that sprouted the root in the girl's mouth. And maybe they did. Maybe I did.

We thought we were helping something, but more truthfully, we were devouring the pain of a people who were more like artifacts to us than humans. We learned to lament the condition of their living, to look on barefooted children and shake our fists in the air, all the while remaining willfully ignorant that our hungers, policies, and histories of colonization and global exclusion were the very things that had hidden them in the cane.

I am sitting on the perimeter of the clearing of a different batey; to my left, the wall of sugarcane, so close I can lean over and rest my head against it. I do not. In the cane, side by side with me, is a boy my brother's age, wearing a tattered flannel over a T-shirt with Biggie's face on it. He breaks off and tears open a stalk and hands it to me before grabbing one of his own, and we're sucking sweet juice from the reeds like vampires. I ask him what he wants to do, and he doesn't understand. I say, *Work—trabajas?* And he points to the field of cane with the top of his head. *Te gusta?* I ask, gesturing toward the fields like I'm cleaning up a mess in the air. He caresses the stalk in his hand, smiles, and says, *Good, I like.* He swings his arm like a bat against the wall of cane. *No like.*

I used to think justice for the land and justice for humankind were two different callings. In the sugarcane, I learned that any separation is an illusion. When Flint, Michigan, didn't have clean water for a decade, the land and creation was suffocating from that same injustice, but that injustice was able to survive for so long precisely because of the people it was tormenting. Their dignity was obscured by our malformed relationship to the earth. When we march for clean water in Flint, we march for its residents. And when we cry justice for the people of Flint, we cry justice for the waters beneath them.

I saw the face of God in this boy. His bondage depended on the land, yet he, in wisdom, was still capable of loving it. Of slurping its juices in delight, gazing out at the sea of green like it was a sunset. He understood that his freedom was connected to the land's, and I cannot say for sure, but I believe he longed for its rest as much as his own. I go back there in my dreams sometimes. It's like my mind can't untangle itself from the stalks. I don't want it to. I want a justice ethic that longs for the healing of both the boy and the sugarcane that imprisons him.

Admittedly, when you are existing in a society that has you working multiple jobs, raising children without help, barely getting by, you cannot be faulted for not having the breathing room to recognize the danger of carbon emissions and microplastics in oceans, or even the water flowing out of your own tap. Sometimes, in order to fight for justice for creation, one has to have one's most basic needs met. It is hard to talk climate change with someone kneeling on your neck. But as we move toward liberation, it is our responsibility to do what we can to liberate everything in our path, even the earth beneath us.

. . .

In Genesis, when God gives Eve and Adam authority over creation, it is not permission to do whatever they want; it's an honoring. It's permission to be the mouth and hands of justice, protectors of every created thing. Over time we've taken this role to look more like domination than cultivation. Instead of resting the land, we overharvest it, we exhaust it. Instead of marveling at the tree, we make plans for its utility. We are a people much more concerned with ruling than loving. This is a mistake that positions us in places where we are no longer close enough to another person or thing to perceive its pain or need. To be human in an aching world is to know our dignity and become people who safeguard the dignity of everything around us.

To protect everything may seem like too great a call. But we will not survive without it. Everything should be called by its name.

So let justice roll down and twist and juke like a movement. Let it march into your bones, into seas of charred cane. Wash the earth in justice and watch what rises to the surface. Curses can't breathe underwater.

ELEVEN

Repair

In the beginning, when all people laughed and wept and danced in one clearing, a searing bright cloud passed over everyone, and for one gaping moment, no one could make out one another's faces. When the cloud finished passing, they looked down and found that everyone's insides—guts and veins and organs pumping and squirming dark—were now on their outsides: a lung soldered to the outside of a neck, retinas turned inside out on foreheads. They were terrified of their own faces, but they soon learned they could get on. They learned to walk differently, suspicious of one another. And everyone kept a bit more distance, because liver touching liver—well, it was agony. Insides were never made to touch like that. Everyone started keeping a bit more distance, until eventually they spread out across all the earth.

I need not tell you how the story ends, because you know what happens when a person becomes so afraid of themself that they become afraid of everything else. When the pain of disorder becomes too great. I wish I could tell you that they all just learned to remember the blinding bright cloud and moved closer to each other, making shields and new skin of their once-nuclei. But you know better than that.

Even if you learn how to walk differently, the soul becomes hungry in the absence of repair. In time, their interiors became like vacuums, sucking back up first their organs, then their blood and guts, but all out of place and twisted together. And when that didn't satisfy, they began snatching up everything else. Leaves from every bush they passed, twigs from the fire, flea and rabbit. And eventually, despairingly, one another.

That is how it happened.

There is no blade of grass, no body, no starlight, that is not in the end begging for repair. This is not poetic despondence, it's a tragedy we must contend with in order to get free. Repair is more than justice. What do we do once the curse is lifted but the damage is untouched? When justice is had and the swords are beaten into plowshares but everyone's wounds are still bleeding in the open, what then? Justice doesn't survive without repair. We have to pause and bandage ourselves up habitually. Even when the oppressor has been defeated, we are worthy of tending to the pain of the past. Repair—truth-telling, reparations, healing, reconciliation—these are what breathe new life into us.

. . .

When I was little, I would never confess to anything. I just answered my father's questions with another question. *Did you kick that ball into the porch light?* he'd ask. *Didn't you tell us not to kick the ball that direction?* I'd say back. Sometimes he'd stare me down until I confessed. But other times he'd just sigh to himself and pull me close. He knew and I knew what I failed to admit to. But those things collect on you like dust, and keep you from the liberation that comes with forgiveness and resolution.

Call it archaic, but I think confession is liberation. It is easy to think that in injustice only the oppressed have their freedom to gain. In truth, the liberation of the oppressor is also at stake. Whether it's the privilege we've inherited or space we've stolen, what began as guilt will mutate into shame, which is much more sinister and decidedly heavier on the soul. It doesn't just weigh on the heart; it slithers into the gap of every joint, making everything swollen and tender. We learn to walk differently in order to carry the shame, but then we become prone to manipulate things like nearness and connection just to relieve our own swelling.

When wounders, finally becoming exhausted of their dominion, dismantle their delusion of heroism or victimhood and begin to tell the truth of their offense, a sacred rest becomes available to them. You are no longer fighting to suspend the delusion of self. You can just lie down and be in your own flawed skin. And as you rest, the conscience you were born with slowly begins to regenerate, and your mobility changes. You walk past the shattered porch light without your nose to the ground. You can look your father in the eyes. You realize there are other ways to move in the world. It's not only relief, it's freedom.

Truth-telling is critical to repair. But confession alone—which tends to serve the confessor more than the oppressed—

will never be enough. Reparations are required. To expect repair without some kind of remittance would be injustice doubled. What has been stolen must be returned. This is not vengeance, it's restoration.

Maybe you know the verse that says if someone slaps you on the right cheek, turn and bare your left cheek to them too. But before all that, Exodus says *eye for eye, tooth for tooth, burn for burn*. Payment, consequence. Any injustice demands something of us. But the only thing more healing than forcing someone to pay is when a person chooses to pay by their own conviction.

I have always wondered why Christ had to die. If we needed saving, if wrath was to be had, couldn't God just snap his fingers or send a great wind or blink and have everything wrong made right again? Why is it *nothing but the blood*? Nothing else? This will always be strange to me.

But if it's true, the law is cosmic and eternal. Maybe it's written into everything, and even God themself is not too bold to undo the way things were meant to be. Maybe they needed to show us what the most tragic and noble reparation could look like, the sacrifice of life itself, so we might learn the courage to choose to make repairs when our moments come.

But some will die in their cowardice.

. . .

My gramma was standing on a balcony in the belly of Maryland when a whistle floated up to her from below. She had dropped out of school and was living in a tiny apartment with a friend. *You wanna come party?* he said. It was summer and hot as hell. *No, I don't know you,* she replied with both irritation and mischief. *What's your name?* he said, heat jumping off of him and rising to meet her. *Man, you're a trip,* she said, still making up her mind. She turned and let a smile slide out from her as she went inside, leaving him to wonder.

Then she slithered into a lime-green jumpsuit and went downstairs. And there he was, sitting on the hood of a red convertible. Skin soft and white, hair combed back like a movie star.

She got in.

The whole romantic scene was deflated almost at once when he, leaning over to her with pseudo-suaveness, spilled his beer all over her jumpsuit. *I didn't like him at all.*

Yet some combination of his persistence and the persuasion of the only friends she had led my gramma to marry this man. *I never loved him. I knew it when I said yes.*

As the allure of her wore off and her unlove became apparent to him, his ego grew so wounded that he began inhaling her secrets and storing them up inside of himself. *Everything I ever told him, he digested and spat back at me.* And when that didn't work, he'd simply flaunt an affair in her face, trying to convince her of her insignificance in other ways.

When the marriage finished crumbling, she moved back to New York and took their three big-eyed children with her. He resented her even more for having the strength to leave, strength he lacked. And his resentment, which he mistook for love, became obsession. He followed her.

He would call again and again. He would show up at her job, which she desperately needed to keep. There he was, outside of her apartment. There he was, chasing her through the subway station. One day he had been calling for hours and eventually showed up outside her door. *Chile, I leaned my head out of the second-story window—in the city we used to do that all the time back then,* she says. *Anyway, I lean out to try to talk some sense into him, and all of a sudden, he's pointing a gun at me. Right at me.*

She spent many years running from this man, moving from place to place, state to state, stretching out the tether between them all the way across the country until it snapped. And she was in California.

Reconciliation is so elusive because so few ever occupy a state of sincere remorse. If we are to be reconciled, the offender must become disturbed by the state of their soul—a contrition that births apology not for the sake of its own forgiveness but to honor the dignity that was once at risk.

When you're little, apologies of *I'm sorry*—or worse still, *Sorry*—are accepted as enough. It trains us for the wrong thing. A few years ago, I reached the conclusion that I will no longer accept an unspecific apology for specific wrongs. If you cut me, I want you to apologize with grave specificity for the blood running down my back. And I want you to describe what in you made you do it. When you gain the courage to look at me, I want your soul to writhe like it was the back of God that was cut. This would make any sorry truer.

A friend once explained to me the second and often forgotten part of apology, which I now believe to be one of the holiest: when one *asks* to be forgiven. Mercy requires nothing from the offender, but to ask forgiveness is to shift the balance of power in favor of the wounded. It requires you to become vulnerable to their denial. For a moment or perhaps many moments, the weight of your soul depends on the humanity of the one you sought to demean. *Will you forgive me? Please forgive me?* These are holy beginnings in pursuit of reconciliation.

One night in California, my gramma was driving home, and she turned and ended up on a hill overlooking all the lights in the valley. *I can't explain it. I just looked out at all that beauty and felt something shift in me. And I said out loud, "Wherever he is, I forgive the bastard." And that was it.*

Forgiveness came to her not in a dramatic flourish or sudden comprehension; rather, it grew on her as slowly and fatefully as the fingernails crowning her hands. You participate in it, it comes from you, but it also is something that happens to you without you necessarily noticing. I don't think we have as much control over our forgiveness as we think. You can't force hair to grow faster than your body allows. I think this is okay. You cannot reason resentment away, nor the trauma that grew it. There is time.

. . .

There are some of us who have grown weary of talk of reconciliation. This is probably because it comes to us on the tongues of men who have paid no time to the process of true repair. It is both ego and shame concealed in shallow unity-speak that regresses any progress that has been made.

And you'd of course be right to ask the question: Can we be reconciled if there was no harmony to begin with? I suppose it is my faith that allows me, despite all the lack I see, to trace the plumb line back to an origin story of harmony—a shalom that can be repaired, however slowly and painfully.

But language of unity has functioned as a locution more of restraint than of liberation. Those who are too insecure to practice an ethic of true repair attempt to accelerate resolution for the sake of their own protection. They are unprepared to fully face the chasm they have created, the blood on their hands, the sight of their own face, so they rush to an assurance that the sight isn't as ugly as it seems.

Reconciliation cannot be forced if it is to last. And unity should not come at the expense of the vulnerable. Its integrity depends upon its ability to make the union safe and honorable. How can you become one with a person or system who will not acknowledge or relent in their torment of you? This is not unity; it's annihilation.

When my gramma first told me about the man who was not her father, and the yellow dress, and the basement, I felt like she was staring into me. *How can you make sense of something like that when you're just a little thing? You just have to remember it's not your fault*. And I look away, but she doesn't. She points to her gut, not mine. *It's not your fault.*

The moment passes then, but one day, over the phone, a pause stretches out between us, and maybe it's easier in this moment because she can't look at me, and that makes me feel safe.

This day, I tell her we are *the same*. I hear her breathing.

I say, *When I was little*. And her breathing stops.

She says, *Who?* I say his name. She says, *How old?* I say, *Little*. She says, *Nicole. Nicole. Look at me*. And I look up at the clouds. *It's not your fault.*

And then, *I'll put a hole through his chest.*

When she was fifteen and the church found out about the child growing in her and how it came to be, there was no such rage. *They rebaptized me side by side with Satan. They put me under with him,* she whispers with a smile. *They said we'd be new.* And the word *new* comes out like an eerie song.

Her church tried to disguise their cowardice in language of reconciliation. But even then, she knew it wasn't for the sake of unity. It was for the sake of him.

Now, ear to ear and miles apart, she makes no such demand of me. The only reconciliation she seems interested in is restoring me to myself. *It's not your fault. Little girl, forgive yourself.*

. . .

In the third year of my sickness, the devil touched my legs, and I was in and out of a wheelchair for a week. We were in Paris at the time. Days before, I had been at the Cleveland Clinic, with doctors furrowing their brows and sighing at imaging of my brain. And the next day, we were on a plane. At first, it just felt like I was walking on legs that had fallen asleep. And then it was like walking as my calves and thighs were being twisted from inside, like every muscle in them had been pulled. When the pain became too much and I could no longer hobble, we began taking cabs and getting a wheelchair every place we went.

I went to the Louvre and saw more butts than paintings. My arms were too weak to push myself, so my husband sheepishly wheeled me around while people towered above me, usually in front of me, blocking my vision. I began cussing people out, first under my breath, then louder. But from that level, and with all the echoes, no one really heard me, or at least they pretended not to.

You wouldn't know it from our photos, but I spent two

days of that trip in bed, my only consolation the *pain au chocolat* and espresso my husband would race back to me multiple times a day, his eyelids dragging with sadness. I was alone in bed that second afternoon when I began to pray aloud. Praying doesn't encapsulate it—I was begging. Flat on my back in the sheets, talking to the ceiling like it had a face. I never begged or bargained so desperately in my life.

I was not healed.

But in those desperate utterings, I saw things I didn't even know lived inside me. I saw the profound hatred for a body that was only doing its best to survive. *Don't make me live with these fucking legs. If you just free me from these hands . . .* I had turned against myself. Once I heard it out loud with such venom, I became suddenly very sorry. And a realization came awake in me: My body was not the bondage.

I lay there in stillness, and like the ancient ritual that precedes the Eucharist, I traveled around myself and passed the peace. I made peace with my eyes, feeling my eyelashes flutter against the back side of my hand. I made peace with my legs, flexing at the ankle and feeling where it hurt. With my trembling hands, and shallow breath. Peace. And I cried a different kind of tears. What once was enemy became the object of my affection and protection.

It felt like a vow.

I don't know if liberation depends on our reconciliation with others, but I am certain it at least depends on our reconciliation with ourselves. In this life, it is all we can do to stay whole—an interior unity. We owe that to ourselves.

The most beautiful thing about the human body to me is regeneration. To stave off the holes in my eyes, the doctor shoots lasers at my retinas to create burns around the edges. And as my eyes heal, the retinas, which they're worried will detach altogether, are welded down to stop the tear. It sounded barbaric to me at first. But as that bright light seared into my eyes, I marveled at my regenerative powers.

We are a people whose flesh grows back. It does not die quietly. We must remember this, even in the most painful conditions of our healing.

. . .

I used to think rehab would change everything. It changes many things but not everything. My family still lost our house. And my father still relapsed. And the fear has never left me.

My father, still hero and still flawed, has been clean for seven years. To me, his healing had no precise beginning or end. A raft bobbing in the ocean without a sail, slowly guided to shore by the mercy of the waves alone. His recovery did not feel at once triumphant. It did not feel like a conquering; it was a restoration. A wounded man restored to himself. And my sweet, magic father restored to me.

I asked him if he felt free now that he was clean. I didn't even finish the sentence before he said, *No. No. You don't feel free, you feel ashamed. It's once you're clean that you remember. You remember and then you start asking, What have I done? How much damage did I do?*

As we heal, the need for more healing becomes apparent to us. It is painful, but healing makes us better perceivers of what is still hurting.

My father's affliction left a thousand tiny scars on every part of him, some that he'll never dare let me glimpse. All I know is that they welded his selfhood back down and delivered him back to me. I am indebted to every mark.

. . .

It's the second July of the pandemic and I'm hunched over her hospital bed. I'm trying to breathe through a mask, and my gramma through plastic oxygen tubes resting in her nostrils. It's the first time we've seen each other's faces since I told her *me too*. She's telling me stories about her childhood but she's using *we* and *you* and *I* interchangeably so I can't quite follow when she is talking about her story or mine. I make no attempts to clarify. I'm stroking her arm. Finally, she just says, *We did good. We did good.* And I'm watching my tears pool between my flesh and hers. *We took the sweetest part of the fruit and we cut it off.*

This I believe. That I come from pain as much as beauty. And I don't have to make the pain beautiful in order to get free. We took the sweetest part of the fruit and we cut it off.

So one day, when you look down and you're wearing your own veins on the outside like a lace dress and everything is tender and everything hurts, wait out the shadow of despair. Do not force down poisoned fruit. Repair is after you, a seamstress in flight to your splitting parts. Feel the thumb of God pressing the earth slowly back onto its axis. *We did good. We did good.*

TWELVE

Rest

Every Black woman is born knowing how to time travel. The first woman to disclose this to me, whether by purpose or accident, was my gramma. She was leaning back in a suede recliner, and I was on the floor plucking up stray fibers like flowers. We were talking off and on while the television hummed in the background. Her eyelids slowly closed as she caressed her own house dress in between her pointer finger and thumb. And I looked up and she was gone.

It took my breath away.

I stood up and slowly approached her empty throne, unsure what I was moving toward. I hovered above the air she left behind. I closed my eyes, and as I started to wave my hand into the emptiness, it met her velvet chest. I opened my eyes, and she was staring at me with a smirk. *Little girl,* she purred out. *What in the hell are you doin?*

I asked, *Where did you go?* She said, *Honey, I'm just resting my eyes.*

To rest is a special kind of power. Even someone who is direly overworked can close her eyes for two minutes and, by the mercy of God, find those seconds stretched out into years, allowing the healing and regeneration she deserves to come in a blink.

It seems like anytime God is talking about salvation in the Bible, he makes a point to name rest. "I'll refresh tired bodies" (Jeremiah 31:25, MSG). "Find rest for your souls" (Matthew 11:29). And, in Psalm 23:2, we have "He makes me lie down." What a peculiar answer to the valley of the shadow of death. You might expect God's response to be to have people rise, to empower them to fight. But God's answer is unapologetic care for the body. The deepest yet most neglected of needs.

What does it mean that in response to the terrors of the world, God would have us lie down? To eat? To drink from still waters? The most enduring yet undermined sentiment of evangelism: "Come to me all you that are weary . . . and I will give you rest" (Matthew 11:28).

Yet when we invite people into spirituality, too often rest is reduced to an inner posture someone should adopt while exhausting their body. But the Bible says, "In returning *and rest,* you shall be saved" (Isaiah 30:15, emphasis mine). If the "salvation" you've been promised requires you to do and say more, you can be rightly suspicious of it. You say *confess your sins.* Okay, and fair enough—but maybe I'm saved a little every time I rest my eyes.

The curse of the world has made for restless hearts, bodies, minds. Our hands fidget, we open and close our emails, we obsess over something we said yesterday. It's like the atoms that make us have begun darting around in and outside of us with no awareness of each other. The current of the cosmos shifted, and now God is trying to steady us and make it so that we can be still without becoming terrified of things, of ourselves.

A peace once stolen, now restored. This is our journey.

The atoms that make up my mind are like the tiny bits of flame that dart off of a sparkler. I envy people like my husband who will tell you more often than not that they're thinking about *nothing*. He can drive a car and let everything go silent in him. He's the kind who can fall asleep while he is literally speaking. For me, falling asleep is a mercy that comes only after about an hour of my soul trying to jump out at me. I've tried to count sheep, but I couldn't count them without picturing something happening to them, some story they were in. This one just had an awful shave. That one is being slaughtered tomorrow. These next two are in love. For all my effort, the night ushers into my body a new form of restlessness.

When you spend most of your days demanding life from your mind, its movement can become a nuisance to any attempt to truly rest.

Perhaps most foundationally, it is fear that keeps us from the rest we are worthy of. A few weeks ago I saw a neuro-optometrist because of issues with my eyes unrelated to my flimsy retinas. She placed her fists together and sent her pointer fingers to opposite corners of the room. *Your eyes are out here.* Then she slowly guided them to meet each other in the middle. *We need to get them back here.* She told me my pupils were massive, and when she shone a light on them, they'd contract for a second and then give up like they were slumping. Turns out my eyes show that my sympathetic nervous system, which triggers things like fight-or-flight stress responses and the release of hormones, is overactivated like I'm encountering a threat at all times. And my parasympathetic nervous system, which is meant to guide me into rest and relaxation, is being held down like a baby bird who is still too heavy to use its wings. So I'm left with giant pupils and my vision drifting outward and my anxiety swallowing me when I hear a loud sound or drive at night.

To treat the condition, they're putting prisms in my glasses to help steady my eyes for me. And once a day, I go into a dark room, put on these strange glasses with blue lenses, and stare at a light bulb they gave to me in a paper gift bag. I get real still and force my eyes to the light as I think about how the restlessness of the world has possessed my body.

Once possessed, we must steady ourselves habitually in order to see the way we were meant to. For some, stillness will not suffice. The stillness must mature into an inner quiet—the noise of the exterior world ricocheting off your flesh. To cultivate habits of rest, we must discern what noise has found a way to penetrate our soul. And as we detect patterns and modes, we have more of a grounding as we resist restlessness.

In this way, the silence of God, which is so often mistaken for abandonment, may be a gift to those of us who cannot steady our souls in the vibrations of the world's clangor. It's a liberation from a world that demands too much of our minds and bodies and whose noise does not relent.

For others, rest is the current which drags us back into stories and emotions that terrify us so profoundly that we have become numb to them in order to survive. Each second of inactivity rouses those stories or emotions, or at least triggers our fear that they will be roused. Stillness, silence, rest—this is much to ask of a person.

Stillness makes for a capable mirror. Look down in a rough and fast current, and you won't see a thing. Still water allows you to lean in without danger and really see yourself. And in doing so, you may remember a liberty over yourself that is easily forgotten when things are jostling you about.

. . .

Rest is not the reward of our liberation, nor something we lay hold of once we are free. It is the path that delivers us there.

In California, the grim condition of my gramma's days became apparent to her. She arrived with my aunt and uncle. They were in high school and knew that this was not a time to complain that their clothes didn't fit and they were still hungry after dinner. With no money and no place to go, they slept in the car. She'd stroll into the grocery store, pay for a loaf of bread but steal the bologna. *I was surviving.*

One evening she was driving and driving around with my aunt and uncle asleep in the backseat, trying to quiet the stress in her head. Until finally, sad and worried about using too much gas, she pulled into a church parking lot to turn in for the night. She was staring through the hole in the floor of the Pinto, picking at herself and dropping tiny bits of skin through it, when a small, leathery man drummed at her window with fingernails like bark. *Ya alright?* And she said no. *Ya got someplace to sleep?* And she was tired and she said no.

He was a pastor. He gave her twenty dollars to get some

food and led them to the quiet of the church auditorium. They slept in dusty folding cots. They didn't stay long because of the roaches. But this benevolent gesture gave her a tragic fragment of what she had been denied for so long—rest. And it gave her the confidence she needed to pursue it for her and her children by any means. She found the courage to stay at a shelter for a month. This was not the rest they were meant for, but it was something.

I have to believe that if we didn't need to protect ourselves, we wouldn't be so prone to avoiding rest. When fear enters the story, something changes.

In response to the risk and need around us, we have constructed systems around labor that leave even the hardest workers vulnerable, in deficit. Labor is no longer a gift. How could it be when one is withering from hunger? Labor instead becomes a means to an end, not an avenue for flourishing but a transaction for survival. This is a grim human development, for no one wants to spend their days merely surviving.

And this transaction is nearly always incongruent with the amount of labor one does. You can work, as my gramma did in California, for a full month just to be able to finally move from the shelter into low-income housing. Meanwhile, the powerful convince us that there is not enough while their pockets spill over out in the open. They distract us from this by dangling *opportunity* in the opposite direction. They appear as rescuers, demanding ceaseless labor from us but presenting it as a gift. We are expected to feel deeply lucky and even indebted to a society that allows us to work, even if that work cannot satisfy our most basic needs.

And it is the specter of scarcity that withholds the rest we have been made for, the paradox being that what feels so much like risk is actually the means of restoration. We sleep and we regenerate. Our cells begin a sacred rhythm of repair and release. And when we wake, we are more healed, more whole, less inflamed, more aware. And, of course, we sleep that we might dream. A balm made of mystery, and it has been kept from so many of us.

There may be the rare angelic parking-lot pastor intervening in the belief that every soul deserves a place to lay their head. But some of us have come to expect exhaustion and enslavement from every soul we collide with. We become used to it, we participate in it, and then we become reckless demanders ourselves.

God, in Christ, learned something of this incessant demand. In one of the gospels, Jesus wakes up at daybreak just to go out to find a place to exhale alone for a bit. The crowds go and hunt him down, and they're clinging to him, begging him to not leave again. Jesus puts them all in check, as if to say, *Don't you know I have other things going on? You are keeping me from my purpose.*

If Christ walked away, so can I.

I sometimes wonder what willpower, what fidelity to rest and waiting it must've taken for God, knowing he had all the capacity and strength to heal every person in every crowd, to walk away. At first it seemed nearly callous, but it liberates me as I create boundaries in my own life.

I see the longing and despair all around me, and I think of Christ, lying in the boat with his head on a pillow while the waves toss their craft around. Everyone is frantic, thinking death itself has come for them, and the creator of the universe is fast asleep. Glory.

Sometimes the appropriate response to desperation is to do the unthinkable. Close your eyes.

. . .

My father, the hustler, never really learned how to rest. He says once he started to believe that if he just worked harder, he could have a little more power over things, it was game over. He says, *I was never the smartest person in the room, but I could outlast anyone. I had to.* This was his path to exhaustion.

He was just a teenager when my sister and I were born. When he was twenty, he became a single father, and the tightrope he was already walking—living paycheck to paycheck, working two jobs to survive—finally snapped. All at once he was falling and tucking our heads into his chest to brace for impact, but by some miracle, God blew his phone closer to him mid-freefall and he caught it. *So I called my sister.*

My Aunt Jenny, my Uncle Dave, and my gramma were all living together in California by then. They said *come.* And he did. When he shut the door of his two-seater Honda Accord, the car made a funny sound, something like an inhale, and leapt a few yards off the ground. And just like that, the steel and rubber reestablished themselves, and we were off. He made the four-day journey in minutes. It was as if his family summoned him and all the atoms of creation realigned themselves for a moment to deliver him back to them.

He sleepwalked into that crowded house. When he woke up

the next morning, my sister and I were in the kitchen with my gramma and aunt making breakfast. He says, *I got up, and my sister looked at me and just said, "Go back to bed. The girls are fine."* And this simple moment stilled the chaos.

He sauntered back to the bed that didn't belong to him and slept for forty days and forty nights. And who could fault him for it? *It was like I had been freezing for so long and finally someone handed me a blanket.*

In community, we can push back on the expectation that we exhaust ourselves. It was no longer my father's lone responsibility to put his two girls to bed or braid our hair every morning. In solidarity, my father's mother and siblings made his sacrifice the sacrifice of the collective. They became harbors, allowing him to find a stability of heart—peace in a maddening world.

I wish I could say my father's peace remained. But anxiety is not a passive predator.

It is awful that what God meant as a gift in the garden—the honor of labor—has become the mechanism by which our bondage survives. I still call my father and beg him to take a day off. But I have become more sympathetic to his plight. He was formed in uncertainty. Uncertain of food, of place, of worth. It does not matter that he is safe now and has enough. The memory followed him. Some remnant of it clings to him even now.

Activist and theologian Tricia Hersey says, "This is literally life or death. It's the matter of whether or not we're going to stop and listen and slow down and reclaim our bodies." She says "to not rest is really being violent toward your body, to align yourself with a system that says your body doesn't belong to you, keep working, you are simply a tool for our production." But this violence has come to be celebrated and rewarded. And now we demand as much from one another as what has been demanded of us.

We are seldom impressed by simplicity, unless it is the kind inflated with theatrics, which inevitably draws attention to itself—capsule wardrobes, minimalism, van life—and still is, in a manner, *doing*. But we fall on our knees at the sight of a man working sixty hours a week for his law firm in the city. We are in awe of the violence.

And we conflate these idols with God himself. We become obsessed with the language of how God might "use" us, never pausing to ask ourselves, What if God doesn't always want to use you? What if sometimes God just wants to *be with* you? We've become estranged from this idea. We would never articulate it as such, but undergirding much of our concept of calling is the belief that our primary relationship to God is anchored in transaction. God resists this.

People think the sabbath is antiquated; I think it will save us from ourselves. When God tells the Israelites to practice rest, he uses the memory of their bondage to awaken them to what could be. "Remember that you were a slave in the land of Egypt, and the LORD your God brought you out from there with a mighty hand and an outstretched arm; therefore, the LORD your God commanded you to keep the sabbath day" (Deuteronomy 5:15).

When we rest, we do so in memory of rest denied. We receive what has been withheld from ourselves and our ancestors. And our present respite draws us into a remembrance of those who were not permitted it. Hersey says that "our dream space has been stolen, that there has been a theft, a complete theft. What could have happened if our ancestors had a space to rest, if they were allowed to dream?" When I rest my eyes, I meet those ancestors and they meet me, as time itself blurs between us. They tell me to sit back. They tell me to breathe. They tell me to walk away like they couldn't.

. . .

Rest is an act of defiance, and it cannot be predicated on apology. It's the audacity to face the demands of this world and proclaim, *We will not be owned.*

We will not return to the chains that once held us. They are brittle and tarnished from our tears, which made the flood. Remember. You were never meant to prove your dignity. You, whose flesh contains more bodies than your own. You don't belong in the catacombs of restlessness, wandering from death to death. Lie down with me in the pasture, where life is alive and growing with the unapologetic slowness of a blade of grass. What will become of us?

We will be free and we will be dreaming.

THIRTEEN

Joy

A tall velvet curtain ran through the center of the auditorium, splitting the space in two. On one side, a mass of clumsy preteens bobbed and swayed to the music. On the other, parents huddled up in clusters, containing all the nerves they'd wished away from their children hours prior. My father was sliding in and out of groups of parents, casting spells to make everyone feel as if they belonged. He'd inhale their tangled insecurities and watch the other person's shoulders relax into place as they collected on his own diaphragm, waiting for the exhale. After a while he settled into a table far enough away from things that he could rest but close enough to still feel the bass from the other side.

It was still a half hour before the dance was over, so he was surprised when he looked up to find, emerging from the other side of the curtain, my sister—bony, Black, and sparkling. There was no distinction between the glow of her flesh and the shimmer of her dress. She came glistening over to him, ducking and shirking through the crowd, her reflection gazing up at him through the overly polyurethaned floors. And he was sitting there holding his breath and smiling, as if to say, *Don't worry about me. I'm doing okay.* But she grabbed his hand like it was a belonging that she'd forgotten and pulled with a force that seemed strange for an eleven-year-old. *Come dance with me,* she said. *I want to show you to everyone.*

And the momentum of her joy collided with his chest at such a rate that the breath he'd been carrying was knocked right out of him. *I don't remember any of the people she introduced me to, but I remember her not being embarrassed of me.*

He says, *People say the birth of your child is the happiest moment of your life. But when your child chooses you . . .* And his sentence doesn't need a close.

Joy, which once felt as frivolous as love to me, has become a central virtue in my spirituality. I am convinced that if we are to survive the wait of justice and liberation, we must become people capable of delight. And people who have been delighted in.

Some of us go our whole lives without ever being—or rather, knowing that we are—truly enjoyed by a person. We can become cynical about communal affirmation, hoping that our affirmation of self will suffice. We try to meet our self-hatred with the sound of our own voice, because this, for whatever reason, is seen as a superior strength. But I think we were made to be delighted in. And I think it takes just as much strength to believe someone's joy about you as it does to muster it all on your own. We shouldn't need to choose self-affirmation at the expense of the affirmation of another. I think we were meant for both. We need both a personal and a communal praxis that actively resists our self-hatred. Sometimes we must declare peace and tenderness over our own bodies. But sometimes we need the sound of another's voice to celebrate us. Joy plays no small part in that.

As our societies tilt more and more toward the shallow images and yearning that social media manufactures so well, we have become rightfully paranoid of public affirmation. Delight in a person can't always be distinguished from flattery.

Even still, public affirmation has the capacity to heal the shame that is awakened in public places—it can help you to relax your shoulders, to exhale. And when others bear witness to that affirmation, their very presence doubles the effect. As you watch them believe someone's delight in you, you become more likely to believe it as well. It opens up the joy so others can partake in it; you see the truth of your own worth in a diversity of faces and expressions.

. . .

My family has always been playful. A joy in action. When my Uncle Dave saunters over to my Aunt Jenny and rests his head on her shoulder, only to light her up with a wet willy. When my father pulls over, turns down the music, and makes the whole car listen to the new rap he just made up, while we're all squealing and reaching from behind to pinch his neck and cheeks. This is a part of our healing.

There are those of us who are such serious people that to be playful feels foolish, and maybe it is. But I think when we give ourselves to play, the scope of our lives expands. We become freer in our bodies. We give ourselves to imagination and make-believe. This takes down our defenses and allows us to move and be without expectation of immediate tragedy. After all, it is only in anticipation of sorrow that joy seems frivolous. We become so used to bracing for the next devastation, we don't have time or emotional energy to rejoice. For some of us, this moves us to a permanent seriousness, always on guard against the evils of this world. Some of us even begin to believe we are not worthy of pleasure or play.

Of my rowdy and mischievous family, my gramma says, *We argue loud, we cry loud, and we laugh loud. We are nothing if not sound. No one is going to say that we weren't here.*

I resented this for some time, thinking this somehow spoke to a shallowness in my family. On the contrary, it has always spoken to a depth.

I was four and my sister six when my father moved us all to Florida. He had once again made his way back to his family—my gramma, Aunt Jenny, and Uncle Dave having already relocated there. We moved into an apartment with my Uncle Dave, and we weren't there for long when my father's car got stolen and money got tight. So tight my Uncle Dave suggested trying for public assistance.

My father was immediately resistant. To be more accurate, he said, *HELL NO*. But even as he was saying it, they were walking to the office on Broad Street, and by the time he finished with his drawn-out *NO*, he was out of line with three hundred dollars in food stamps. He tossed it to my Uncle Dave like it was something contagious.

Don't you know, my father shrills out to me not as a question but a confession, *I had that little book of bills for days, but I was too embarrassed to spend it.*

But my Uncle Dave was like, *Maaaannn, forget that, I'll spend that shit.* And they rolled up to the supermarket. At first my father was nervous, his heart in his throat. But my Uncle Dave started goofing around and making a show of everything. *Nigga, we gettin steak ta-night.* And he throws the steak in the cart. *We gettin all these eggs, how many eggs you want?* And he jukes over to him. *Nigga, we ain't about that skim milk, we splurgin on WHOLE milk today.* And he plops one down in the cart.

My father says they went cuttin up all through that store. And he's cracking up as he tries to tell me about it now. When they finally got to the counter and my father's shame reappeared, my Uncle Dave snapped out the book of food stamps and started plucking bills out theatrically. *And what do we owe you?* he said, as if he were prim and polished. With a cart spilling over, they expected to have to pay more than the stamps could cover, so when the woman said $185, they let their knees go weak and start cracking up even harder. The whole store turned to look at them, two golden-skinned boys hanging on to each other, play-punching each other in their bellies and letting the howls echo between them.

We're talking about relief. It was food, and it was such a relief. But it was more than that, he says. *It was fun as hell.* And he's still smiling.

It requires attunement to practice humor without violence. You have to acquaint yourself with insecurity, people's stories, and the needs in the room to bring levity into their heaviness without diminishing their pain. But done right, humor can hold together seams under the harshest duress.

On that day in the grocery store, my Uncle Dave turned my father's shame into joy. When you find people like this, don't let them go.

. . .

My gramma says you'll know it's joy when you feel it in your entire body.

She was swaying in a sea of candlelight when it happened. Under a canopy of string lights and stars, her family stretched out across the wooden tables. She looked over, and I stood there in the distance with my father, my ivory gown swept under me like I was walking on a chiffon river.

He had his hands on the sides of your face, and you just stood there for a bit talking like that. I swear that moment fused to me. There was my baby, talking to his baby. And I was sitting at a table with people who liked me. Who love me. She sat and watched my uncle and aunt poking each other and warning each other with their eyebrows. She watched my sister and cousin whispering to each other in between selfies—the little girls laughing and safe. *And it just hit me,* she says. *These people came from me.*

And, *I was in and outside of myself at the same time.* Maybe this is the heart of joy.

The psalmist says:

> When the LORD restored the fortunes of Zion,
> we were like those who dream.

Then our mouth was filled with laughter,
    and our tongue with shouts of joy;
then it was said among the nations,
    "The LORD has done great things for them."
The LORD has done great things for us,
    and we rejoiced.

Restore our fortunes, O LORD,
    like the watercourses in the Negeb.
May those who sow in tears
    reap with shouts of joy.
Those who go out weeping,
    bearing the seed for sowing,
shall come home with shouts of joy,
    carrying their sheaves. (Psalm 126)

Joy, in this song, is inherently communal. I like that the translation says "our mouth," not "our mouths," as if it is one collective mouth laughing and crying glory synchronously. And here the joy of the Israelites was rooted in memory. "Those who sow in tears." "Those who go out weeping." Almost as if their capacity to lament was what awakened the joy in them.

That is not to say that those who have lived painful lives have access to more joy. (It may certainly be the case, but of this I am unsure.) But it is to say that those who refuse or neglect to tap into the sorrows of the world may find joy elusive.

There is so much that is worthy of lament, of rage. Joy doesn't preclude these emotional habits—it invites them. Joy situates every emotion within itself. It grounds them so that one isn't overindulged while the others lie starving. Joy doesn't replace any emotion; it holds them all and keeps any one of them from swallowing us whole. Society has failed to understand this. When it tells us to find joy in suffering, it is telling us to *let it go*, to *move on*, to *smile through it*. But joy says, *Hold on to your sorrow. It can rest safely here.*

My gramma's deepest experiences of joy come in moments when it feels as if something has been restored or renewed. When repair happens, we must bear witness to it. Joy does that. It trains us toward a spirituality that isn't rife with toxic positivity but is capable of telling the truth and celebrating when restoration has indeed happened. Gratitude doesn't disguise the curse, it celebrates what the curse hasn't touched or marred altogether. As we experience restoration and healing, joy is at once our memory of the bondage that once was and an honoring of the liberation that has come.

With my flushed cheeks between his honey palms, my father says, *I only want for you to have more than I did*. And I know by his eyes he is talking about more than money. *You're gonna be okay. I'm so happy, honey. You're gonna be okay.* My family says my wedding night was the best night we've had together. In part because we Arthurs haven't had many weddings (so no one can get offended if we name mine our best) and in part because on some shared plane of the soul, we recognized that it was as much theirs as mine.

We were like those who dreamed. Despair and pain can steal our imaginations. Under twinkling lights and the dark of an oak tree, we reclaimed ours.

. . .

I don't believe there is a soul who has known me who would say *happy* is one of my defining characteristics. My gramma says, *You know, you were always a solemn child.* My father says, *I could read anyone like a book, but not you.* He says it's because everything I say has a little bit of sadness in it. Something indecipherable.

We are driving home from Red Lobster and everyone is crammed into the car. I have a window seat and my little brother's head is toppled over on my shoulder. The music is loud, and my stepmom's foot is on the dash. And my sister is singing the song out like she wrote it. And my father is looking over his shoulder at me, and he's saying, *Why are you crying?* And I shrug as I keep my eyes on the window. *Nicole, what are you crying for?* And I do not know.

For the most part, this has remained in me. Years later, I would be diagnosed with depression and anxiety, which to me didn't mean much, because the only self I've known has been laced with sadness and fear. To name it was not a revelation, but I did feel seen.

I was driving home to my basement apartment outside of Philly, the first place I ever lived alone. No one was waiting for me, so I always took the long way. I must've driven past it a hundred times—a tiny gravel lot on the side of an unremarkable road. It couldn't hold more than two cars at once, but it was always empty. And that day, I held my breath and cut across the lane of oncoming traffic and landed there. I got out and the gravel led me to a reservoir. It was enclosed by a line of trees. A rock dam had been kissed all over with graffiti. I wasn't looking for a sanctuary, but it did something to me.

There, on the edge of a rock, hidden in plain sight by still water, I found an ineffable contentment. Something about the simplicity was liberating to me. I had been around the world. I had knelt before its wonders and many times felt nothing at all. But this was ordinary beauty. And maybe the smallness of such beauty made its joy easier to access.

I called it my secret spot. And I brought everyone I could there. I wanted them to have a piece of the secret.

I once heard that joy and happiness do different things to the body. Happiness, which works itself out in the sympathetic nervous system, makes you excitable and energetic. It's important but fleeting, grounded in the immediacy of a moment or the whim of a feeling. Joy is more tranquil. It has to do with the parasympathetic nervous system, and it's much more about peace than vibrancy.

In this graffitied, man-made, ordinary reservoir, I found some manner of peace.

For some, contentment bears the risk of complacency. But there is a contentment that can be active in the world. This can be a joy that still dreams, but it dreams in peace, not in terror.

I wouldn't have articulated this, but I think I've always believed my depression disqualifies me from joy. I don't know how to quell the ache in me; I have not known a day in a long time when I wasn't aware of it on some level.

Marie Kondo famously told us to pick up a possession, and if it sparks joy for you, keep it. If it does not, let it go. I once heard her say that you know it's joy when you feel your body-soul lift up, even if only slightly. Not joy, and your body-soul slouches within itself just a touch. I wonder if we were to lift our own selves up, how many of us would end up throwing ourselves out along with bread ties and the jeans that don't fit us? My soul is often slouched. I would not survive the purge. Thankfully, we can assume Kondo would discourage applying her method to people. But it compels me to ask the question: What is the worth of a woman plagued by sadness?

When people demand *joy always*, it makes the world seem incompatible with those of us whose happiest days are still anguished. In this way, joy was one of my earliest alienators. If I did not belong to this loud, laughing family, whose was I? I was the child who would sit in closets or bathrooms while everyone else laughed together in the kitchen. Every now and again, someone would knock and whisper through to me, *Well, you gonna join us, hunny?* But I'd stay tucked away under Goosebumps books and shadows, knowing I was never going to laugh like them.

It took time for me to realize that it was not that my family wanted me happy; it was that they wanted me close. They didn't want for me the kind of sadness that alienates you. In time, I learned how to be in the kitchen, and it didn't seem to matter if I was laughing. My sister pulls me close and feeds me a bite of spinach dip. *Just stay with me.*

Depression may contain a joylessness, but it doesn't have to. When we reimagine joy as more than mere happiness, we make space for a sorrowful joy. Mine is a joy born not of laughter but of peace. This is okay.

Scholar and theologian Willie James Jennings said, "I look at joy as an act of resistance against despair and its forces." Despair does not want to see us reach the promised land. It does not want us to find belonging in our families, or peace down by the reservoir. Our liberation depends on our willingness to resist it. We do this by allowing joy, in whatever form, to be our song.

There's a moment in the Bible when the temple of God, which was destroyed during the exile, is being rebuilt. The Israelites lay the foundations, and a lot of the people begin shouting for joy. But many of the elders, those who had known the former temple, wept. They remembered what was. Ezra says, "No one could distinguish the sound of the shouts of joy from the sound of weeping, because the people made so much noise. And the sound was heard far away" (Ezra 3:13, NIV).

I have not found a better portrait of joy. Sorrow and celebration all mixing together in a holy cacophony. A collective so loud that weeping and laughter were made one. A sound so loud that it was heard by others, even those far away.

. . .

As joy gives way to dreaming, our hope becomes more and more secure. We begin to believe that what is will not always be, that the ache will not always linger. And we may even begin to believe that we are worthy of what we are hoping for.

You deserve more than the despair that stalks your days. You don't have to make a sound; just let the peace pass through your belly and be what you need it to be. These terrors don't own your dreams. Call out to the masses, invite them into the warmth of your delight. Say:

> come celebrate
> with me that everyday
> something has tried to kill me
> and has failed.
>
> —LUCILLE CLIFTON

FOURTEEN

Memory

I am sitting cross-legged in a village near Kitale when Lucy comes near and stands over me. She says, *You*—and lets it hang in the air for a second—*are Kenyan*. I force out a laugh and say, *No, American*. And she points at my chest with her whole head before I can even get out the words. *No. Ken-yan,* she says with the queer syncopation of a tambourine, the syllables left clanging in the air long enough to be remembered.

She sees a sadness in me, so she pulls me up, grabs me by the chin, and moves it around like a theatrical inspection. *You. Are. One of us,* she knells out in a whisper. I begin to cry. I try to tell her I don't know where I'm from, not really. And she says, *You don't have to know. I know.*

Lucy was not the first to express this. I had been there for almost a month, and since my first day, I would greet people and they'd stare at me for a second like they couldn't remember where they knew me from. They'd keep hold of my hand like a book you're not ready to turn the page of yet, and they'd just stare. *Kenyan,* they'd eventually say with a release.

At first it felt like the honor it was. I felt at home in a way my two older white male companions did not. It felt like the universe was winking at me every time someone grabbed my hand and let the air hang above us for a moment. That is, until the last week, when we were in the market and two women rushed over to ask me something, but as they got closer, and before I even had the chance to speak, one shook her head no and the other crossed her hands in the air like she was defeated. *American,* one said to the other. And they scurried away like I was a wrong turn.

A simple exchange, but it disrupted something in me. The charade of my homecoming was exposed. I was confronted with the truth, which is that I do not know for certain where the origins of my home are. No memory can take me there. And in that market, I was lonely.

And now, Lucy. Before she leaves, she flings her arms toward the ground. *Don't forget it.*

The oldest stories of where I come from have been stolen from me. I am still grieving the loss and the sense of belonging this disrupted in me. The answers to the biggest questions we have about identity, story, and God can only be answered in relation to memory. Without memory, we are forced to rely solely on ideas and suggestions to make sense of who we are, as opposed to the concrete.

Still, it is not unusual to want to wish our own stories away. To discard the painful ones, the humiliating ones, and preserve only triumphs and satisfaction. But liberation cannot be found by tearing holes into oneself.

People say in heaven we won't remember any of the sorrow anymore. I hope they're wrong. It would be a disingenuous eternity to exist without all that has made me. I hope when God brings heaven down, they bring with them the storytelling circles of old—that we would all gather around the fire listening to the ancestors, singing familiar songs.

I don't want to make it to the promised land if it means I forget the wilderness.

. . .

Even though she couldn't have been older than four when she was sent to live in Pennsylvania, my gramma says she remembers *the before days*. She remembers her Pa Paw making bacon before going to work. He'd flap it down on a castle of paper towels and they'd watch the grease overcome it, forming a moat. And when he was done, he'd go to check on her Gram in bed, but not before turning to the little ones with a bit of mischief in his eyes and saying, *Yin kids betta not touch that bacon*. And as soon as he left, they'd charge the paper towels and run off with their salty loot. This she remembers.

She remembers the face of her mother. A face like wood, only the carpenter got up and walked away before getting to her left eye, leaving the socket raw and empty. She'd place a bandage or patch over it, sunglasses over top, allowing her right eye to live in the shade as well. My gramma doesn't remember her with her glass eye, only the emptiness, which she never mustered the courage to peer into.

Though once her cousin got brave and looked. He stood there staring down the cavern right into the dark of her skull—he said he heard something calling him by his name from inside. And would you believe me if I told you, right then and there, an eye tore out of his abdomen and started darting around? From that day forward, whenever Cousin Beau inhaled deep enough, he saw my great-grandmother's memories. *Seven children hover around a lone can of Spam. The smell of lavender and lemons. A hook reaches into the dark.*

Memory is meant to be given. It isn't held well alone. It is meant to be held in a collective and across generations. Memories that remain exclusive to a particular individual or even community are at risk of becoming false. The smell of lavender becomes the smell of grass. The abduction of Black bodies becomes their "migration." When memory endures no scrutiny or curiosity or challenge from the exterior, it can lead to a profound loneliness at best; at worst, individual or collective delusion.

There are many instances when memory is unable to be held on to. By age or trauma or lack of revisiting, we can lose track of our own stories.

My gramma's blackouts started when she was around twelve. She tells me, *They were so complete, so intense in their absence.* She'd be sitting at the dinner table and then all of a sudden become stunned and confused about how she got there in the first place. One time she woke up and an entire chunk of her hair from root to tip had turned white. *I didn't remember a thing.*

She doesn't forget anymore. She says now she always remembers. *And sometimes that's not a good thing.*

When my friend's father, who has Alzheimer's, forgets a face or loses his place in time, I have always found it so tender that my friend does not immediately correct him. Sometimes, he'll just stay with his father in whatever memory he is able to occupy. This is solidarity. Other times he'll choose one or two details to bring into focus at a time: *You're a good dad. You make the best French toast.* Memory is frail. It requires a delicate touch, a tenderness.

Even those of us who are not prone to forgetting need this. Sometimes, it is only in the hands of another that a memory can be fully encountered. All of a sudden it is not the front of the car you see but the street from the back side window. The memory expands past two dimensions. This is the beauty of collective memory.

Collective memory requires that we piece together the fragments of individual memory and behold something not necessarily *larger* but with greater depth and color. I think the whole Bible is predicated on collective remembrance. You have feast and fast days, storytelling, and most conspicuously, the Eucharist. A shared table and a shared loaf. *Take, eat, drink.* The Christian story hinges on a ceremony of communal remembrance. This should train us toward an embodied memory. My hand on a ballet barre, and every muscle knows how to come awake again. My father takes up my detangled hair in his hands, and his fingers dip and twist so fast they blur and become one. *Do this in remembrance of me.*

. . .

How will we make space to hold the memory of the collective?

There are times when belonging is not cemented in the lived moment of an experience but in the lively or somber retelling of the moment afterward. Which means we can transfer belonging to the next generation by welcoming them into memories that they (or we) have not lived but choose to steward.

In many spaces, to foster collective memory well, we must habitually ask ourselves, *Whose story gets told, whose story is believed, and who gets to tell it?* If we surrender our individual egos, these questions can function as a pruning process, as we contend with accounts that don't line up quite flush. This interrogation may reveal false memories.

When my gramma was in her sixties, she got an email from the wife of a man who was her son. The child made by her and the man who was not her father was found. Or rather, he found her. Turns out, when my gramma went to college, the man and woman went back to the family she thought would raise the child and reclaimed him. He grew up thinking his mother left him on the church's front step. He grew up thinking his mother was a heathen who left him, when she was really fifteen and trying to save him.

My gramma met him. He started coming to Thanksgivings and family gatherings for a while. She tried. I believe she tried. *But his face. He looks just like him. I look at him, but I'm not seeing him.* The memory of the man clung to her. *How can you be a mother to the same face that haunts you?*

She told him the truth of him, but I cannot say if he came to believe her. He'd heard a different story all his life. These things cannot be easily undone. I am not quick to blame him.

The truest memory is rarely the one that survives. In most of our contexts, intellectual, charismatic, white, heterosexual, cisgender men will carry some weight subconsciously as keepers of the history. It is important to name this tendency, for it has been systemically ingrained in us by societies that value their wealthiest, most visible, or most power-possessing members.

Theologian Miroslav Volf once said, "I think the truthfulness of remembering is part and parcel of the justice of remembering. . . . Why do we need to remember truthfully? Because every untruthful memory is an unjust memory, especially when it concerns relationships, fraught relationships of violence between people." In this way, communal storytelling can be an act of justice.

And we must examine how we choose our historians. The story of how the community selected its first leader will be decidedly distinct depending on the vantage point of the historian. When the role is shared by a diversity of voices, the process of curating stories becomes truer and more just. And when practiced well and often, this habit of curating collective memory can not only preserve community but also, in the darkest of moments, resurrect it.

. . .

This is the story I know by heart: My father was just a little boy, and he was playing in the street when his father walked up and said he was coming with him.

He says, *Go on and get in the car.* And my father starts to walk to the car but stops just short of it to bend down and tie his shoe. His father yells up to the apartment and my gramma leans her head out of the window in a sigh, and he looks up at her and just says eerily, *Stephen's gonna come stay with me for a while.*

And my father is just finishing tying his shoe when he hears her: *Run. Stephen, run!*

And he doesn't even look over his shoulder before he takes off.

And he chased me. His father chased him all the way to the baseball field and straight through the middle of a pickup game. *There I was, running from my own father without having a clue why. Maybe I didn't know what I knew.* The knowledge of both his belonging and his endangerment running through him like the sound of static on a TV with no signal.

At the height of the chase, my father trips and falls, and his father gains on him, but as he stands back up, my father twists over his shoulder and all at once flings his bright red baseball cap at him. And the brim of it must crack his father right in the face, because the distance between them doubles after that. He sees a fence and climbs it. He knows his father can't follow, so they both just stand there staring at each other. Pacing back and forth. And his father says, *Stephen, I'm your dad.* And my little-child father says, *I can't.* And then he runs home.

When he gets there, the cops are in their living room, and everyone is all panicked. But my father just waltzes in wordlessly, sits down on the couch, puts his feet on the coffee table, and says, *He was never gonna catch me.* And he feels like he is both the hero and the defeated.

He wanted to go back to look for his ball cap. If he'd found it, he would have kept it forever. He has told the story many times, never quite remembering he's told it to me before, and I'm afraid I haven't yet grasped the weight it has held in his life. I wish I had the ball cap too. He always slows down when he's describing the ball cap—an artifact of his sorrowful salvation. I want to hold this memory with him as long as I can.

To have artifacts that possess our memories maybe makes

it so a memory doesn't sit so heavily on us. It grants memory a body, something physical that you can grab hold of. I think this helps a person to feel in control of their past. But it also makes it so that others can bear witness to the memory themselves, experience it in their own way.

When a person or group has no artifacts to reconstruct their stories, things slip away across generations. People slip away.

Whenever I see old things in antique stores, I think of all the artifacts that were stolen from me when my ancestors were taken. I can travel and imagine what comb they may have used, what their jewelry looked like, but I will never know for sure. I will never hold those things and keep them and give them. This is a tragedy.

For those of us who are trying to carry all our memories on our own and pass them clumsily from one to another, we must learn to create our own artifacts, sacred items of story and existence that have once been denied to us.

An artifact is a little piece of defiance. To say, *I was here. I existed, and this thing happened, whether you believe it or not. This cap right here. Feel the brim.*

This is a form of liberation—to be able to carry your own memories as you choose, to own them.

The Bible says Samuel erected a large stone so everyone would remember that God had protected them. He named it *Ebenezer,* which means "stone of help." And every time someone would walk past it, it was a reminder that God was for them, that God had protected them and would come to their help.

It's not the only time. God tells Joshua to set up stones of remembrance to mark the time when the Jordan River stopped its flow so that they could get across it. The Bible says the whole nation crossed and not one foot got wet. Joshua tells them that when their children ask what the stones mean, they must always stop and tell them the story.

I wish I could build an Ebenezer in Inwood Park. Or one step off of Cemetery Lane. Reminders of all the stories that made me. Maybe in the apple grove next to my sinking barn, in remembrance of a home lost, now found. When my children pass it, they'll ask me, *What are these stones all about?* And we'll sit there, dodging falling apples as I tell them how God once held up the whole sky for me. And I'll watch them eat the fruit that no one will ever take from us.

. . .

Three years ago, I began collecting stories before it was too late. I was sitting next to my father in the car and staring at his hands when it occurred to me that I had never stared at them at all. It's difficult to explain precisely what struck me about this, but it was in that moment that I resolved to begin the long task (or, more rightly, the long habit) of collecting.

I interviewed him first. It lasted three hours. I made sure it was on video so my children's children would not just remember the stories but remember *him* telling them. The way his small hands cut through the air in meaningful arcs. His pursed lips. The eye rolls. Every grin laced with shame. Some of him, of course, will not relent to be preserved on video. I hope those are the things that find themselves preserved in me.

Few would deny that storytelling is core to what it means to be human. Perhaps this reflects something of our maker. God asks us in more ways than one to remember—to "put the Lord in remembrance" (Isaiah 62:6, ESV®), to "do this in remembrance" (Luke 22:19), to "tell your children of it, and let your children tell their children" (Joel 1:3).

When Hagar runs away from a household of enslavement, abuse, and neglect, she meets an angel of God in the desert who asks her, "Hagar . . . where have you come from and where are you going?" (Genesis 16:8). A question to which I suspect God already knows the answer acutely. Yet it is asked of her. Then God explains what they know of her story and what her role in the cosmic story of liberation will be, and tells her to return to where she had come from.

I mostly despise this story. It seems cruel that Hagar, who has known such alienation and suffering, would be expected to return to her oppressors only to endure more. And that her lineage would be destined to exist in tension and struggle. But I am learning to attune myself to Hagar's words in the story. Hagar names God "the God who sees" and says she has "truly seen the One who sees me" (Genesis 16:13, NLT). Hagar's story reminds me of the profound healing that can occur when someone is given the liberty to have their story held, their suffering named. To belong to a God who asks, *Where have you come from?*

Maybe God knows the paths we've walked, but there is glory and healing in watching it fall from our own lips, in our own words. We must relearn to embody a holy story exchange. Memory is not just to be held but to be told—and this is especially true in a world where we are so often refused the right to tell our own stories. Part of the power of remembrance is in its recitation. When we lose someone, one of the things we're asked to do in grief counseling is to tell what the person was like, to tell a memory of them. It doesn't matter that the counselor has likely never known the person; there is healing in the telling.

Traditionally, Western Christianity has replaced Christian habits of storytelling with singular and all-encompassing testimonies of a person's conversion to faith. This is sad to me. We must recover a habit of very specific story exchange and shared memory if we are to have robust liberation.

. . .

First, I interviewed my father. Then my stepmother. Then my grandmother. I prompted them with questions, but eventually each story began to drag another to the forefront as it departed. I wasn't looking for them to verify each other's stories. Most shared memories did seem to line up; at other times, things became . . . tangled. Not only dates and names, but pretty significant disparities in the plot. *Who left whom? And what do they believe about why? Who believes in God?* Some stories only come to us in fragments. I'm beginning to believe that is the beautiful way.

After I finished listening to my gramma, she cupped her head in her own shoulder and asked, *You got what you're looking for, babygirl?* Perhaps she sensed a desperation in me. We are desperate for knowledge of self, but even more, we are aching for the stories that have made us. We dare to touch the histories of this world, knowing that in them we are brought into a collective. If it's freedom you're after, who will show you the way? Whose memory guards the secret paths? Remember and tell it.

FIFTEEN

Liberation

One day, at the end of all things, the legs of all the tables in the world will come alive. And without apology, they'll each begin plodding toward the space where the top and bottom of the earth meet. And we'll be terrified, of course, so some of us will go into hiding underground, but some, after pausing to feel sad or terrified or betrayed, will get brave and follow them. Those who are able to withstand the pilgrimage, who are able to push back despair in the company of the tableless, will make it to where they're going. And when they arrive, they'll find all of the moving tables lined up into one great plank tracing the entire equator.

The children will sit first, because they are unafraid. And the elders will follow, because they are unafraid of their fear. And eventually everyone will take a seat, squirming their elbows in tight. Some will be grunting, complaining about how absurd the whole thing is. Some will be laughing, in awe of how beautiful it is. And some will be crying, sensing how familiar it all is. And in mystery, and all at once, we'll look up from the table. And we'll see ourselves. At that moment, the wood of the table will begin to suck all the shame out of the air, and once it does, the air will become so light that we all will realize how little we've been able to move in our own bodies before this moment.

When we understand that the food is not going to fall from the clouds or manifest from the knots in the table, we'll take ourselves and begin wandering off to collect things. And we'll probably get lost now and again, but the table will just send out a long whistle and lead us back.

I believe that the individual, collective, and cosmic journey is the path of unearthing and existing in our liberation. But liberation is not a finality or an end point; it is an unending awakening. It is something we can both meet and walk away from within the same hour. Our responsibility to ourselves is to become so familiarized with it, so attuned to its sound, that when it calls out to us, we will know which way the table is.

To answer the question of how one becomes attuned to liberation, I think we must ask ourselves: What sounds are drowning it out?

. . .

This is what I haven't told you. I'm four or five and my hand is stuck in the space between the sliding glass door and the screen door, and my father is in the living room with my Aunt Jenny and some people I don't remember the names of, and nobody sees me. I know I need to ask for help. I want to scream, but I don't. I wait. I try to will my father's eyes to me. I tap the glass with my forehead but it bends the screen into my fingers, which are crying out, but I am not. My tears are quiet and fall unnoticed for I don't know how long until my sister sees me and helps me pry the door open with our little-girl muscles. She sits me down in the shade of our swing set and says, *I'm coming back*. And when she does, she's carrying a fistful of freeze pops and a half bag of frozen pizza rolls. She wraps them and a row of the pops around my throbbing hand, except the blue one, which she leaves out for us to split. *You gotta say something.* I don't. She says, *We're gonna scream, okay?* And she counts to three on her fingers, pressing them against her lips like she is first saying, *Quiet*. And then she lets it out, alone at first, but I get brave and join her. *Again!* And our squeals pierce the glass. Inhale. *Again!* And the whole house comes running.

When I was little, I didn't speak. This is not an exaggeration. Apart from the family who shared a home with me, I was nonverbal around most people I encountered until I was about seven. It's called selective mutism, and it's an anxiety disorder. Even after seven, I was a very quiet child. A quiet adolescent. It wasn't until college that I really started speaking a lot, trying to mirror the girls who seemed deep and charismatic and beautiful to me. I started rambling and rushing out words like a dam in me had broken. I became "social." For a year, I was witty. Fast. Until I didn't recognize myself. They said I was *blooming*. They said I was *opening up*. But what looked like freedom was pretending. And it was exhausting.

When we were little, my father used to have us write poems and little stories to get out of chores or as competitions in the car. He bought me diary after diary and never asked what I was writing, only *if* I was writing. Maybe he knew that freedom for me would not come as a loud and triumphant metamorphosis. A little girl bent silently over herself and her purple pages. *Tell me a story, babygirl.*

My soul will probably always contain more quiet than sound. Liberation, for me, was learning how to scream when I want to and then silently pass the freeze pop back and forth between slurps. It was knowing the sound of my own voice. It's the sound of these pages.

· · ·

There will always be people who are threatened by freedom in another person. Who have something to gain from our bondage.

And there are also voices who deeply love us but are unable to exist in the tension of who we are and what we believe and who they desire us to be and what they desire for our beliefs. This is the life of a human, particularly a human with any concern for belonging or survival—we are dragged with such a force in so many disparate directions that our souls, disoriented, are unable to find their way back to center. And for most of us, the journey back is costly.

In spirituality, this leads many of us to profess beliefs that we do not truly believe. Like when I told a cabin full of campers that if they confess their sins and believe in Jesus, they'll be saved from hell, when really I don't know what hell is or if I'm going or if I've been. Or when Dae tells me she likes girls and I sit in silence instead of saying, *Me too,* and it's terrifying, but if there is a God, I hope he loves us not despite this but because of this.

Many of us end up surrendering a spirituality that allows

us to be curious and uncertain and free so that we can maintain some semblance of belonging, even if that means we adhere to a way of life that doesn't leave room for the truth of us.

Whenever I become uncertain of which direction liberation lies in, I ask myself to tell the truth. Not that I am capable of comprehending what any ultimate Truth is. But I am capable of at least telling the truth about what I believe to be true—my inmost convictions, desires, or even an embodied revelation. The truth that rattles in my bones.

There is no greater exhaustion than a charade of spirituality.

A life that is holy is a life that allows for all of your uncertainties, your curiosities and unbelief. That doesn't just allow for them but holds them as sacred. Spirituality that is not permitted these liberties is merely subjugation. It is not in protection of the divine; it is in protection of fragile people who are unable to allow spiritual freedoms without their own spirituality feeling threatened. It's a spirituality that is terrified of meditation for fear of resembling another faith tradition. It's a spirituality that spends more time on apologetics than conversation and telling stories.

To be liberated spiritually is to commune with and seek God without fear of alienation if we do not reach the same conclusions as our neighbor. It is to become spiritual creatives.

Who are we that we would demand certainty or clarity of mystery?

In too many spaces, we've become suspicious of beliefs that leave room for the unknowable. If uncertainty is permitted, it is permitted around carefully defined points of interest. Like Communion. Or mortality. There is rarely room for new uncertainty. If one person is certain about a thing, it demands, either in agreement or disagreement, a certainty (or feigned certainty) from all others.

Perhaps you have hung on to this book in hopes that I would reveal a truth to you. Maybe some will close this book, exhale sharply, and ask themselves, *What did this teach me?* If the answer occurs to you immediately, I believe I have failed. I hope any truth I've written unfolds slowly, encountering you first as what I, Cole, believe to be true in this particular season. And as you go about your days, I hope you find familiar fragments in your own stories and contemplation, whether they're in alignment with or contrary to mine. I am not threatened by this.

. . .

If we have any interest in representing a liberating spirituality, we must adopt a spiritual psyche whose deepest concern is not enlightenment or education but doing our best at telling the truth.

A person who has the wrong answer but believes sincerely that they've found the right answer is nearer to truth, and perhaps God, than the person who says the right answer but in their soul believes it to be wrong.

Liberation erects a bridge between the unreal and the real. Between the little girl who once lied about having friends in school and the girl who years later cries and laughs into her sister's lap admitting she will never be like her. When we encounter ourselves on the shore of the unreal, together we implement new habits of self and communal compassion, and patience, and inclusion, so that we can safely travel into what we really think and feel. It requires that we tell the truth—or rather, what we believe to be true in the season of life we are in. Even if our voices are shaking. Even if we're dead wrong.

We can and should empathize with how long this journey can take. For some, it may seem as easy as summoning our true selves and choosing to unveil them to the world around us. But this is a risk. What becomes of a Christian who is uncertain that Christ is divine? What becomes of the hero who says, *I am no longer interested in saving this family*? The truth is, when I let myself be quiet again, people were no longer drawn to me in the same way. As we bare all aspects of our true selves, we become vulnerable to all manner of rejection, leaving us raw and sending us back into a deeper hiding than before. I think every act of fidelity to a truth in you is an act of liberation. It takes time for people to feel true in their own minds and bodies, and even once they have, I'd suggest the experience still ebbs and flows as a person expands in their own flesh.

I think we can be fully free yet still have the capacity to become more free. Maybe this is heaven.

. . .

I asked my father to tell me a story about a time he felt free. It might've been the first time in my adult life that he didn't call me with an answer within the hour. I waited for days and checked back in. I waited a bit more.

Finally, I call and ask him why he thinks it's so difficult for him to locate a memory of freedom.

He says, *Free? I guess one day.*

He explains that he has always felt a weight, a pressure building in the air around him. He is always worried about something. Right now, it's retirement and if he'll ever have enough to rest. But also, the memories of his worst moments and decisions haunt him. I can feel him raise his eyebrows through the phone. *Yeah, I'll feel free one day. When I rob that Bank of America around the corner. Shiiiiit.*

We laugh, but we know there is a weight between us now. We both understand what he is naming is a tragedy. We hang up the phone, and I still feel it. Lacking the courage to call back, I send him a text—and perhaps it's better written, an artifact of our repair. I write, *I'm proud of you. And I forgive you. And I'm certainly not ashamed of you.*

I don't know if my father felt any freer reading those words. Maybe he'll read them over and over, letting his liberation build in him like a muscle. I hope.

You can't talk someone into their liberation. Telling someone to just get free is like telling someone to stop grinding their teeth in the night. It is not kindness. Freedom requires patience with ourselves, as it takes time to feel at peace if all you've ever known is insecurity. It's the process of your soul learning to trust again—trust that it can rest and love and be still without being destroyed.

When someone has endured bondage for so long and has still found some manner of survival, they may assess the risk of liberation to be greater than the violence of their chains. The clang and weight of our iron can even become forgettable as our tolerance for it grows. We can write songs to our chains without ever realizing what's making that sound.

This is never to be demeaned—when you've gone without food for so long, your stomach becomes used to smaller portions. If you've gone without a roof over your head, once you have one you may be less inclined to tell the landlord it's leaking.

In *Beloved,* Toni Morrison famously writes, "Freeing yourself was one thing, claiming ownership of that freed self was another." She nods toward a process by which our liberation is both found and operated within. You may very well find the Table, but when will you take the first bite? Will you look up and really see yourself?

To have the audacity to be and love and know yourself in a world content to have you live your days in hiding—this is bliss.

This allows you to move in the world in a way that isn't jealous of other people's freedom but desires it for them. You begin to crave it for those in your midst, because liberation loves company. It is not threatened by another person's identity, because liberation is not a scarcity. It can only affirm itself in another person.

. . .

The Bible tells the story of the daughters of Zelophehad—Mahlah, Noa, Hoglah, Milcah, and Tirzah. In their time and place, when a man died, his sons would inherit his property. But Zelophehad had no sons, so when he died in battle, his daughters went to Moses and all these male elders and demanded that they get the inheritance. When I tell this story to people, they, rarely acquainted with it, say something like, *Wow, what came over them?* Or remark at how bold they must've been. They are more than this. Mahlah, Noa, Hoglah, Milcah, and Tirzah—these were women who knew their worth. And they stood in power in front of the powerful because of it. They didn't sulk around waiting for someone to recognize their worth, they walked in it.

Moving in your liberation does not, of course, mean people will always recognize it. God told Moses, *You better give those women their inheritance.* And it was given. But we do not know what would've happened in the story without the voice of God.

Still, the very act of the daughters of Zelophehad believing in their dignity and demanding their inheritance conferred freedom on them. Our liberties can certainly be supported and protected by the world, but a form of freedom can still be attained otherwise.

. . .

In the days leading up to her departure from Cemetery Lane, my gramma's skin began to molt. When she told them she'd be going to the Seventh-day Adventist school in another state, things got bad. *When I tell you they whupped me . . .*, my gramma scoffs. The first time she brought it up to them, it was the wooden spoon. The second, a russet potato slipped into an old sock. She admits now that in some twisted way, this was the first time in her life she felt wanted. *If they hated me all like that, why were they so mad when they could finally be rid of me? It don't make no sense.*

She packed the day she was leaving, and fast. And her molting had developed so that large velvety swaths of skin came hanging off of her, and she began accidentally folding them in with her wool sweaters. When the hour came and they all realized she was really prepared to leave them, the man who was not her father began pacing around at the bottom of the stairs. *With his gun in his hand, always with his gun.*

The bus station was twenty miles away, and she was prepared to make a run for it and hitchhike, but the angel from church who'd helped her enroll in the school flew over, and my gramma hopped in the car. And the man who was not her father—needing in that moment to play the part of the man who was head deacon—wasn't going to shoot nobody in front of the angel.

She sat in the station in her dusty little oxfords and bobby socks, skin raw but now soft as ever. She said she just knew they were coming after her. *I couldn't take my eyes off the door.* And when she boarded the bus, she just knew they'd come bursting through the doors and haul her kicking and bloodied back to where she belonged. But when the bus lurched backward and then took off, she knew she had made it. She felt her whole soul relax. *I thought, No matter what happens out here, I'm not there anymore.* The bus sped away with her freed flesh flapping in the wind. And she was born.

When the woman who was not her mother died, she—out of guilt or remorse or even cruelty, we do not know—left the house to my gramma. My gramma wanted nothing to do with it.

People didn't understand why not—why, even if she did not want to live there, she didn't sell it or give it away. She says the process was too great and too painful for her. She says it'd be different if it were a place she loved. *Please—why would I wanna pass on a curse?*

I'm very skeptical of generational curses. I don't think they mean what we think they mean. We speak of them as if they are inevitable, as if they've already latched on to us and our job is to reverse them. I once knew a girl whose parents wouldn't let her sleep over at someone's house if their parents were divorced. They talked about it like it was an omen. We think we are inheriting a curse, but really we are inheriting stories, which it is our responsibility to make sense of and lament and rage against and heal from. More often than not, if a curse is awakened, someone roused it.

For those whose ancestors bore great evil into the world—which may very well be all of us—the curse is only passed as you participate in it. It is our responsibility to know and own the stories that have made us in such a way that we forsake the curse. This requires a sacred humility, for humans quite readily accept their place in the glories of their ancestors but remain woefully unwilling to accept the connection to their ills. But it is precisely our failure to acknowledge the curses we've benefited from that keeps us from full liberation.

A curse is no more inevitable than our liberation. And it is available to each generation in its own way. My ancestors may not have possessed the same freedoms as I do, but who am I to say they were any less liberated? If you take liberation to mean that my ancestors could do everything that white people could do without enduring violence, then maybe. But is this all liberation means?

Author bell hooks said, "Women's liberationists, white and black, will always be at odds with one another as long as our idea of liberation is based on having the power white men have. For that power denies unity, denies common connections, and is inherently divisive."

In pursuit of liberation, we do not need to pine after the power of our oppressor; we have to long for our own power to be fully realized. We don't want to steal and dominate someone else's land; we want agency in reclaiming and establishing our own spaces. We don't want to silence the voices of our enemies; we want to be able to safely center our own voices and be believed. Liberation recognizes that I won't get free by anyone else's bondage.

I believe my ancestors knew things about freedom I can't even begin to articulate myself. Maybe liberation is not as linear as we assume. Each generation may seem more liberated, but there are always new forms of bondage—virtue signals, digital radicalization, activism perverted by a disordered appetite for influence. It is much better, then, to learn what freedom sounds like. Just because you've found it once doesn't mean you will never wander again. We must teach our children and our children's children what it means to be free. What it feels like to be whole. To exhale. And stories are our greatest teachers.

. . .

I know a woman who, when just a little girl, was terrified of her basement. Until one evening, she grabbed her blanket and pillow and marched downstairs and declared to her parents she would be sleeping in the basement that night. They let her, and she slept there all the way until dawn. And she said she wasn't afraid after that.

The last step of my basement was like ice, and I sat on it. I rested my laptop on my lap and bowed over it like a prayer. And I read the first chapter of this book aloud. It was one of those things I did before I could fully articulate why. It did not feel as theatrical and profound as it now sounds.

I listened to each word fall from my tongue and ring out in the most magically mundane way. I wish I could tell you the dust danced and sparkled before me like flecks of gold. It did not. I coughed a lot, and my eyes burned and watered.

When I finished, I sat there for a while and watched the sump pump suck up the water that had collected from the storm. Then I got up and went back upstairs.

My father and gramma don't live in houses with basements anymore. My descent and ascent was for all of us.

People think liberation is a future unfolding before us. But the path to freedom stretches out in both directions. It is what you've inherited, your first and last breath. Walk backward and graze your gramma's face, unshackle your father from the bathroom floor. Go ahead and cry, flip the table, and then repair it in time for the feast. If it's freedom you're after, go marvel at the sky, then look down at your own marvelous hands. Rest your souled body with another sacred body and tell each other the truth: Your dignity cannot be chained.

ACKNOWLEDGMENTS

I am made of gratitude when I think of all those who are tied to this book.

My gramma, Phyllis Marie, whose words were the genesis of my own, but who passed before she could read these ones. I don't want Thanksgiving to come without you. And, I believe you.

My father, Stephen, for building a home of stories. I'm glad to belong to you.

Wallace, my husband, who believes in my words more than I do. Thank you for making the best of a partner whose most profound thoughts strike at midnight.

Char, my stepmom, for crying at nearly every beautiful thing I've brought into this world. My sister, Tanasia, for showing me what courage is. My brother, Ricardo, for being one of the earliest conduits of laughter in my life. For Shakur, the little boy who stirred a healing in me. And the rest of my wild and mischievous family, including my mom, Kimberly; my siblings Cherry, Chay, Teria, Cody; and my Aunt Jenny, Uncle Dave, Queen Kendall, Charlotte, Maddie, Aunt Kathy, Michael, Tatyana, Pierre, Lincoln, and Reese.

My mother-in-law, Sue, whose intellectual brilliance is matched only by her commitment to service. You have shown me what it means to be both head and heart. And to the late Charles W. Riley, a father-in-law who never gave up trying to draw me out of myself. Peter, who edited the sample chapter of this book on a moment's notice. And to all of my other thoughtful, bridge-loving in-laws: You are people of relentless welcome. I'd choose you again and again and still.

My editors, Derek Reed and Ashley Hong, for helping me to say the truest thing, and having mercy on me when I am helplessly meandering in the abstract. I have seen myself more clearly by your curiosities and belief. And the rest of the Convergent team for advocating for this book and leveraging creativity and thoughtfulness on my behalf, including the book's talented cover designer, Sarah Horgan.

Rachelle Gardner, my literary agent, who knows what words are worth and gives me the gift of watching a woman do her job with unapologetic advocacy and competency.

The readers and keepers of Black Liturgies, through whom I have found the healing required to write publicly and honestly again.

TN, for being a friend who inclines my heart toward wonder and mischief. Schug, for telling me the hard truths and staying. Cody, for showing me how to live into my full freedom of selfhood. Esther, Abby, and Natalie for being my own personal three Fates, speaking miracle after miracle into existence, including this book. And all other friends whom I have learned from and who have held me in this process, including Heather and Ivan, Michael and Rachael, Andrea and David, Tommy, Jamie, Rimes, Rich, Derrick, Dante, Candice, André, and Karl and Julie.

The Chesterton House staff team, who have given me mercy, care, and affirmation as I write and also work full-time.

My church and rector, who know more than most what a difficult season I've written this book in, and who never missed an opportunity to drop off food or flowers or toys or books in support of us.

Byron and Beth Borger of Hearts and Minds bookstore, who gave advice freely as I was discerning the book-writing process early on. Your work and resourcing is a gift.

The students who have loved me even as I've failed them. So much of this book was me learning the sound of my own voice as I spoke to you.

Toni Morrison, James Baldwin, Howard Thurman, Julian of Norwich, Dietrich Bonhoeffer, Simone Weil, Lucille Clifton, and Thomas Merton—who have mentored me from the grave.

BIBLIOGRAPHY

Baldwin, James. *Notes of a Native Son*. New York: Penguin Books, 2017.

Balthasar, Hans Urs von. *The Glory of the Lord: A Theological Aesthetics*. Edited by Joseph Fessio and John Riches. Vol. 1, *Seeing the Form*, edited by John Riches. San Francisco: Ignatius Press, 1982.

Bonhoeffer, Dietrich. *Life Together*. Translated by John W. Doberstein. London: SCM Press, 2015.

Cleaver, Eldridge. *Soul on Ice*. New York: Dell, 1991.

Clifton, Lucille. *The Book of Light*. Port Townsend, WA: Copper Canyon Press, 1993.

Coates, Ta-Nehisi. *Between the World and Me*. New York: Spiegel & Grau, 2017.

Dickinson, Emily. *Selected Poems*. Edited by Jackie Moore. Oxford: Oxford University Press, 2006.

Fujimura, Makoto. *For the Life of the World*. Directed by Evan Koons. Acton Institute, 2014.

Hersey, Tricia. "Resting on and for the Earth." Interview by Brontë Velez. *Atmos,* April 28, 2021. https://atmos.earth/rest-resistance-colonization-black-liberation.

Hersey, Tricia and Ayana Young. "Rest as Resistance." *For the Wild,* June 8, 2020. Podcast. https://forthewild.world/listen/tricia-hersey-on-rest-as-resistance-185.

hooks, bell. *Ain't I a Woman: Black Women and Feminism*. New York: Routledge, 2015.

Jennings, Willie and Miroslav Volf. "Theology of Joy: Willie James Jennings with Miroslav Volf." Yale Center for Faith and Culture. Recorded August 21, 2014. YouTube video. https://www.youtube.com/watch?v=1fKD4Msh3rE.

Julian of Norwich. *Revelations of Divine Love*. Translated and edited by Barry Windeatt. Oxford: Oxford University Press, 2016.

Lorde, Audre. "The Uses of Anger: Women Responding to Racism." In *Sister Outsider*. New York: Penguin Books, 2019.

Merton, Thomas. *Love and Living*. Edited by Naomi Burton Stone and Brother Patrick Hart. Orlando: Harcourt, 2002.

Molina, Pedro X. "The Complicated Risk: An Interview with Pedro X. Molina." Interview by Nicole Arthur. *Sampsonia Way,* July 25, 2020. https://www.sampsoniaway.org/literary-voices/2020/06/11/the-complicated-risk-an-interview-with-pedro-x-molina.

Morrison, Toni. *Beloved*. New York: Vintage International, 2019.

Perkins, John M. and Rick Warren. "Loving Jesus in a Fractured World." Sermon. *Loving Like Jesus in a Fractured World* series. Saddleback Church, January 7, 2018. https://saddleback.com/watch/loving-like-jesus-in-a-fractured-world/loving-jesus-in-a-fractured-world.

Rustin, Bayard. "Bayard Rustin." *Book of African-American Quotations*. Edited by Joslyn T. Pine. Mineola, NY: Dover Publications, 2011.

Shakur, Assata. *Assata: An Autobiography*. Chicago: Lawrence Hill Books, 1999.

Thurman, Howard. "The Sound of the Genuine." Commencement speech, Spelman College, May 4, 1980. https://www.uindy.edu/eip/files/reflection4.pdf.

Van der Kolk, Bessel A. *The Body Keeps the Score: Brain, Mind, and Body in the Healing of Trauma*. New York: Penguin Books, 2015.

Volf, Miroslav. "The Justice of Memory, the Grace of Forgetting: A Conversation with Miroslav Volf." Interview by James K. A. Smith. *Comment*, December 1, 2015. https://www.cardus.ca/comment/article/the-justice-of-memory-the-grace-of-forgetting-a-conversation-with-miroslav-volf.

Walker, Alice. *In Search of Our Mothers' Gardens: Womanist Prose*. New York: Open Road Media, 2011.

———. *The Color Purple*. Orlando: Harcourt Brace Jovanovich, 1992.

Weil, Simone. *Gravity and Grace*. London: Routledge, 2004.

———. *The Need for Roots: Prelude to a Declaration of Duties towards Mankind*. Translated by Arthur Wills. Boston: Beacon Press, 1955.

PERMISSIONS

All Scripture quotations, unless otherwise indicated, are taken from the New Revised Standard Version Bible, copyright © 1989 National Council of the Churches of Christ in the United States of America. Used by permission. All rights reserved worldwide. Scripture quotations marked (ESV®) are taken from the ESV® Bible (The Holy Bible, English Standard Version®), copyright © 2001 by Crossway, a publishing ministry of Good News Publishers. Used by permission. All rights reserved. Scripture quotations marked (MSG) are taken from The Message, copyright © 1993, 2002, 2018 by Eugene H. Peterson. Used by permission of NavPress, represented by Tyndale House Publishers, a Division of Tyndale House Ministries. All rights reserved. Scripture quotations marked (NLT) are taken from the Holy Bible, New Living Translation, copyright © 1996, 2004, 2015 by Tyndale House Foundation. Used by permission of Tyndale House Publishers, Carol Stream, Illinois 60188. All rights reserved.

Grateful acknowledgement is made to Copper Canyon Press and The Permissions Company for permission to reprint the following: Lucille Clifton, excerpt from "won't you celebrate with me" from *The Book of Light*. Copyright © 1993 by Lucille Clifton. Reprinted with the permission of The Permissions Company, LLC on behalf of Copper Canyon Press, coppercanyonpress.org.

ABOUT THE AUTHOR

Cole Arthur Riley is the creator of Black Liturgies, a space for Black spiritual words of liberation, lament, rage, and rest, and a project of The Center for Dignity and Contemplation, where she serves as executive curator. Born and for the most part raised in Pittsburgh, Arthur Riley studied writing at the University of Pittsburgh. She once took a professor's advice to write a little every day, and has now followed that advice for nearly a decade.

colearthurriley.com
Twitter: @blackliturgist
Instagram: @blackliturgies

ABOUT THE TYPE

This book was set in Sabon, a typeface designed by the well-known German typographer Jan Tschichold (1902–74). Sabon's design is based upon the original letter forms of sixteenth-century French type designer Claude Garamond and was created specifically to be used for three sources: foundry type for hand composition, Linotype, and Monotype. Tschichold named his typeface for the famous Frankfurt typefounder Jacques Sabon (c. 1520–80).